# QUESTIONS
## EVERY SELLER
# MUST ASK

# QUESTIONS EVERY SELLER MUST ASK

> ## HOW TO AVOID COSTLY MISTAKES AND SELL YOUR HOME FOR MORE

# NEIL JENMAN

## with ALEC JENMAN

WILEY

A catalogue record for this book is available from the National Library of Australia

*Registered Office*
John Wiley & Sons Australia, Ltd. Level 4, 600 Bourke Street, Melbourne, VIC 3000, Australia

For details of our global editorial offices, customer services, and more information about Wiley products visit us at www.wiley.com.

Wiley also publishes its books in a variety of electronic formats and by print-on-demand. Some content that appears in standard print versions of this book may not be available in other formats.

Trademarks: Wiley and the Wiley logo are trademarks or registered trademarks of John Wiley & Sons, Inc. and/or its affiliates in the United States and other countries and may not be used without written permission. All other trademarks are the property of their respective owners. John Wiley & Sons, Inc. is not associated with any product or vendor mentioned in this book.

*Limit of Liability/Disclaimer of Warranty*
While the publisher and authors have used their best efforts in preparing this work, they make no representations or warranties with respect to the accuracy or completeness of the contents of this work and specifically disclaim all warranties, including without limitation any implied warranties of merchantability or fitness for a particular purpose. No warranty may be created or extended by sales representatives, written sales materials or promotional statements for this work. This work is sold with the understanding that the publisher is not engaged in rendering professional services. The advice and strategies contained herein may not be suitable for your situation. You should consult with a specialist where appropriate. The fact that an organisation, website, or product is referred to in this work as a citation and/or potential source of further information does not mean that the publisher and authors endorse the information or services the organisation, website, or product may provide or recommendations it may make. Further, readers should be aware that websites listed in this work may have changed or disappeared between when this work was written and when it is read. Neither the publisher nor authors shall be liable for any loss of profit or any other commercial damages, including but not limited to special, incidental, consequential, or other damages.

Cover design by Wiley
Cover image: © johavel / Getty Images

Set in 11/16 pts and Utopia Std by Straive, Chennai, India.
SKY10152525_041026

*For*
*SACHA KEPREOTIS*
*With appreciation for your kindness*
*and admiration for your competency.*


*And, as always, for my darling wife,*
*REIDEN JENMAN*
*whose love, loyalty and support never wavers.*

# CONTENTS

# DETAILED TABLE OF CONTENTS

# INTRODUCTION: IT'S TOUGH TO BUY, BUT SELLING A HOME IS WHERE BIG LOSSES HAPPEN

In 1976, I bought my first home in the Sydney suburb of Drummoyne. The cost of that home (a small, one-bedroom apartment, but a 'home' nevertheless) was $28 750. It was less than my annual wage of $30 000.

I sold that apartment in 1982 for $71 000. I doubled my money in six years. I thought I was really clever.

Recently, the person to whom I sold that tiny apartment re-sold it for $855 000.

But I'll wager that the person who bought it for $855 000 was not earning $855 000 annually. It now takes almost 10 years of wages to buy an average home in one of our major cities.

There's no doubt that baby boomers had it easier as far as price-to-earnings were concerned.

The story of the struggle for home ownership is a story told daily in the 21st century. Buying a home has never been tougher. And yet, to their credit, millions of Australians strive to attain that dream. They want their own home, and they will do all they can to get it.

Even just to get a foot on the bottom rung of the steep property ladder will be good enough — for now. Later, when their equity increases, they can sell and trade up to something better.

Yes, today's focus is all about buying. But what about selling?

# Selling our home

For some reason there is little or no focus on how to sell real estate. It's because prices are now so high that today's home sellers are almost likened to lottery winners. It seems so easy. Every week, there are headlines about how homeowners are selling for millions of dollars.

And yet, like so much that occurs in the modern real estate world, there is a yawning chasm between the perception and the reality. Especially when selling homes.

Here's a hidden real estate fact. Most homes that are sold these days (especially those sold by public auction) are undersold. Sometimes by hundreds of thousands (even millions) of dollars.

And what's worse is that the owners (those lucky folk who appear to be 'rolling in it') rarely realise they have undersold.

I have spent my entire working life in the real estate industry. Since selling my own real estate office, I have written and lectured extensively on real estate for more than 30 years. I have studied it relentlessly.

My research tells me that the average home is undersold by at least 10 per cent.

Given that the average home price is now $1 million, this means that the average home seller is missing out on (losing) at least $100 000. That's more than a year of the average wage.

What does it matter, you may say? Sellers are already getting huge prices; why worry about getting even more? Is there no end to their greed?

But consider this: *Is it greed to want to sell your biggest asset for the best price?*

If you had $1 million in your bank account, would you withdraw $900 000 and tell the bank to keep the other $100 000?

Of course not.

Well, neither should you leave money behind when you sell your home. No matter when you bought your home, it is seldom easy. Earlier generations paid lower prices for sure, but they also paid higher interest rates (pushing 20 per cent at one stage).

Whether we are buying or selling our homes, every dollar counts. When buying a home, we watch our costs ever so carefully.

But when selling, we are lured into believing we are lucky to be doing so well.

Many people these days sell their homes for, say, $3 million, without realising that, in some cases, they could have sold for as much as $4 million.

This is why there is now a surge in the number of 'flippers' in the property market.

## Beware of the 'flippers'

As you will read in this book, flippers are people who buy homes under market value and then re-sell them, often immediately, for their true market value.

Some flippers are now charging thousands of dollars to teach wannabe instant millionaires how to be flippers. 'Give up your job!' yells the headline in the marketing pitch for the flippers' courses. 'Let us show you how to make two or three hundred thousand dollars out of just one flip'.

'Why work?' they urge. Yes, why indeed.

One of the biggest targets of these flipper vultures are aging baby boomers: those who paid a few hundred thousand dollars for their homes 40 or more years ago and don't fully understand that their homes are now worth a few million dollars.

No matter who you are or when you bought it, your home is likely your greatest asset. Its true value is this: the best price at which it can be sold today. But I repeat, most homes are undersold. On high-end homes, sellers are often walking away without realising they have left millions of dollars on the proverbial table.

## Sharing the secrets of selling well

When I owned my agency, I often saw myself as a teacher for home sellers. I studied the art of negotiation. I discovered that so much of what agents commonly do is wrong. Oh sure, it helps them to make sales. But rarely for the best price.

I realised that public auctions, for instance, were an absurd way to sell any home. I showed sellers what I had learned in auction school, especially how sellers' heads are spinning and how they can be pressured by agents into making instant decisions without realising they have massively undersold their homes.

I showed sellers how too much advertising — or indeed *any* advertising — could massively damage the value of their homes. And, most importantly, I showed sellers how to discover the highest price that buyers were willing to pay for their home.

Today, in this book, I share with you, the homeowners of Australia, what I have shared with homeowners and agents all over Australia in the past 30 or more years.

What's most exciting about this book is that, to the best of my knowledge, it's the *only* book that focuses entirely on how to *sell* a home. There are dozens of books on how to buy a home. But none on how to sell a home. Until now.

Many years ago, a wealthy property investor–cum-dealer told me: 'It takes no brains to buy real estate. Any fool can sign a contract and get a loan. But it takes real intelligence to figure out how to sell a property for the highest market price'.

I am not saying it's foolish to buy a home and get a loan. But I am saying that the questions and answers in this book will help you to sell any real estate for the highest possible price with the lowest stress and without needless costs such as ineffective marketing.

# Where did the questions originate from?

The questions that I answer in this book come from hundreds of questions that thousands of sellers have asked me, my son Alec and our supporters at our vendor advocacy service, Jenman Support, over many years.

They are not necessarily questions for you to ask an agent; they are just questions you need to ask yourself. The answers will enable you to walk away from the sale of your home with tens — even hundreds — of thousands of dollars more than would otherwise have happened.

# What you will discover in this book

Don't undersell your greatest asset. If you sell your home for less than it is worth, you are giving money away. Why not sell your home for its true value and use the extra money for your family instead of buyers who are likely strangers? You can sell your home for more and then give the extra money to charity if you wish.

Or maybe you can help your loved ones to get their feet on that property ladder.

This book will show you how to sell your home for a much better price than you will get with most agents. It will show you how to control agents instead of having them control you. What you do with the extra money you receive because you learned how to sell your home for a much higher price is up to you.

I just hope you don't lose it by underselling.

All I want is for you to sell your home for the right price. And the right price is the best price available in the current market.

As you'll surely discover in this book, that best price is far more than you realised.

Good luck to you.

*Neil Jenman*

# PART 1

# INTRODUCING THE REAL ESTATE INDUSTRY

Your first problem as a home seller is likely that you've got little or no experience in dealing with the many tricks and traps in the real estate world.

Your second problem is that your home (especially your family home) is likely your biggest asset. And yet, as you will see, most home sellers do not get the best price when selling their home. To make matters worse, most sellers also pay too much in needless expenses.

When it comes to experience, most agents have the drop on you. They sell and buy homes for a living. As many sellers discover — often when it's too late — most agents are working for themselves, not for you. They want a sale, sure. But at what price? And at what cost?

There's an old saying: 'When a person with experience (the agent) meets a person with money (you, the home seller), the person with the experience will get some money, and the person with the money will get some experience'.

Don't get your experience through short-selling your home or paying too much in expenses.

This first part of the book will give you a better understanding of the real estate industry. It will also show you how tough it can be for even well-meaning agents to act honestly. Most importantly, it will give you crucial knowledge that most home sellers lack.

And, as you'll see, knowledge can be just as good as experience.

## Questions in this part

1. Why do most people distrust real estate agents?
2. Why is dishonesty common among real estate agents?
3. How do honest agents work in a crooked industry?
4. Why are most agents always short of listings?
5. What is meant by 'conditioning'?
6. What is meant by 'flipping' a property?
7. How do I make sure my home is not flipped?
8. What does 'Don't sign anything' mean?

# 1 Why do most people distrust real estate agents?

The facts are clear. Respected research shows that 95 per cent of people do not trust agents.

Do agents deserve to be the least trusted businesspeople?

Well, yes... and no.

Each year, thousands of decent people enter the real estate industry. Most want to be honest and hard-working.

These good people with good intentions all face the same reality. The *real* real estate world. What they witness often shocks them. Deceit on a grand scale. Selfishness unlike anything they've experienced. At first, many rookies think it's a mistake. Surely their first days cannot be normal. Things must improve.

But no, the more they work, the more disillusioned they become. Until one day — usually within their first couple of weeks, a month at most — they realise that they face an unpleasant choice: stay or quit. Some change agencies... and then discover that the new agency is a clone of the previous one.

If they stay in the industry, they have little option but to fall into line. To do what many agents do: mislead and deceive. Their survival in the industry demands it. There seems no other way.

As new agents soon realise, to be totally honest is extremely difficult. The industry is built on a hotbed of selfishness and greed. This is why the real estate industry has a huge turnover of staff, especially sales staff, most of whom leave in their first year.

To be sure, the industry has many well-honed excuses to explain its bad reputation.

According to many agents, most troubles in real estate are caused by home sellers. Yes, those owners who want too much for their homes. The common thoughts of many agents are: 'How else can we list homes unless we overquote the likely sale price to homeowners? And how else can we sell them unless we underquote the likely sale price to homebuyers?'

All agents know that deception is rampant throughout the real estate industry. And sadly, that's why real estate agents are now the least trusted of all professionals.

# 2 Why is dishonesty common among real estate agents?

Here's what most consumers don't realise: 'selling real estate' is not about selling real estate. It's about *listing* real estate.

Nothing matters more to an agent than listings — that is, having homes for sale.

Unlike people in most businesses, agents can't buy stock. Warehouses don't stock real estate listings. Agents must find their listings. This is why homeowners are bombarded with requests from agents asking if they want to sell. Flyers in letterboxes, phone calls, letters in the mail and, as a last resort, for determined or desperate agents, knocks on the door.

Having found homeowners who want to sell, the agents then face their hardest task: convincing owners to list with their agency.

In real estate, there are no second prizes. Many owners interview at least three agents before deciding with whom to list. The agent who wins a listing usually pockets at least $20 000 — sometimes more than $100 000 — yes, for selling one house. Agents who come second or third get nothing. The most common reason that agents 'get the listing' (as it's called) is because of price.

Here is a common statement to agents from sellers who've chosen a different agent: 'We liked you, but the other agent quoted a better price'.

That's known as 'buying the listing'.

Most sellers ask agents two questions: 'How much is my house worth?' and 'How much is your commission?'

It's only human nature that sellers — especially those with scant experience with agents — select the agent who quotes the highest sale price and offers the lowest commission.

To understand agents, it's important to understand what they face.

Let's say they visit a homeowner who's thinking of selling. This is what's called 'doing an appraisal' or, more accurately, a 'listing presentation'. And let's say the true value of a home is $2 million. Most homeowners — human nature again — overestimate the value of their homes. Perhaps the owners hope to sell for as much as $2.5 million. Certainly, they don't want to consider anything below $2.2 million clear (after commission and costs).

The honest agent tells the prospective sellers the truth: that their home is worth 'around $2 million'. The agent may make the mistake of being more truthful and give a price range; for example, 'This home is worth between $1.8 million and $2 million'.

The owners, quite understandably, are upset. Some are horrified. Others have trouble disguising their anger at what they see as the agent's stupidity.

The agent is shown the door.

A second agent arrives. This agent is vague. Despite being asked several times, the agent dances around the issue of price. Eventually, the frustrated owners say goodbye to this agent too.

Enter the agent we'll call Larry (or Louise) the Liar. Larry smothers the owners with praise and platitudes. While such obsequiousness may be nauseating to an observer, the owners lap it up. Why? Because not only does Larry tell them how much he loves their home, he also says that he has several buyers on his books who will love their gorgeous home. And just wait until he gets them all together and lets them 'fight it out'. Just watch how the price soars into the stratosphere under Larry's negotiation skills.

And the price?

The owners — now quivering with excitement at having met such a magnificent agent — are anxious to hear Larry's estimated selling price.

'Well, who knows? With a home as beautiful as yours, under the right conditions with plenty of exposure, it could reach $2.5 million. Even $3 million would not surprise me.'

But then Larry drops what naïve sellers seldom notice: a foretelling of the future. He introduces the get-out-of-strife card used by dodgy agents: 'the market'. It's the market that ultimately sets the price.

Six weeks later — when the sellers have been conditioned with low offers and sad news — the auction day arrives. Bidding stops at $1.75 million. The owners are speechless. Near tears.

And then Larry pulls a trick used by dodgy agents. The Stimulate Trick. As the auctioneer calls a temporary halt, the crowd fidgets. Larry tells the sellers, 'Look I know it's not what you wanted, but often there are buyers who won't bid until a property reaches its reserve [true]. So, if you lower the reserve now to the amount of the highest bid, it may encourage shy buyers to start bidding. Now's your chance. It may be your last chance to get a decent price. Homes that get passed in at auction often sell for less later on [true]. I don't want you to regret this chance'.

With the eyes of the crowd upon them, the owners crack. Larry points at the auctioneer and yells, 'It's on the market'.

The auctioneer makes a show of attempting to milk more bids from the now bored crowd, many of whom also feel deceived given that Larry was underquoting the home to them and saying it 'could go as low as $1.5 million'.

Suddenly, the auctioneer yells 'Sold!' The buyers smile sheepishly. The sellers look sick.

The auctioneer encourages the crowd to clap. Most obey.

And back in his office the honest agent (who told the sellers the truth about the price at the appraisal all those weeks ago) thinks, 'I could have got at least $100 000 more'. And given that most buyers in most areas are known to most of the agents, that's surely true.

All real estate agents know an awful truth about winning listings: *The biggest liar often gets the job.*

# 3 How do honest agents work in a crooked industry?

With great difficulty. Indeed, employed agents face relentless pressure to use systems that suit the real estate agency. They are told to obey orders. Do what the boss says or leave. Many — especially the decent and honest ones — walk away.

Unfortunately for those starry-eyed rookies who enter the real estate industry, most bosses refuse to consider any methods other than those already used by their agency — and, most stupidly, by their competitors. Therefore, there are only two ways that an honest person can enter the real estate industry and maintain their integrity. First, make the career-endangering choice of defying their bosses. Or second, open their own agency.

# 4 Why are most agents always short of listings?

Because most agents are short on aptitude.

Of course, few (if any) agents admit their incompetence. Instead, they devise excuses to justify lack of stock. They blame 'the market' with comments such as, 'Vendors are holding off at the moment'.

The most pathetic agents try and give credibility to their ineptitude by saying, 'All the agents are short of stock'. Sure, we all lose together.

The real reason agents are always short of listings is because most agents are nearly identical in their sales pitch. Their main difference, therefore, is just their rate of commission. This is why sellers often make the mistake of choosing the agent with the lowest commission rate instead of the agent with the highest negotiation skills.

With the near 30-year boom in property prices, two other things have boomed: the rate of commission and the number of agents. This means that in many areas, there are not enough listings to go around.

But that's just another excuse.

> *Agents who genuinely put their clients' interests ahead of their own interests always have plenty of listings.*

And they are always unpopular with most other agents.

# 5 What is meant by 'conditioning'?

Conditioning is a well-used real estate technique. It means giving home sellers lots of feedback—mostly negative and often frightening—with the express reason of persuading them to lower their price expectations. Or 'meet the market', as agents call it.

Conditioning is caused because most sellers want too much money when their homes are first listed. And most agents feel they need to overquote the price of homes to win the listings.

So, once agents acquire new listings, they must convince sellers to lower their price expectations.

And so begins the 'conditioning'.

Most new agents are taught 'how to condition vendors'. One training book provides agents with a 'conditioning checklist' with 11 main points (or 16 for auctions). Many agents send sellers a series of pre-prepared conditioning letters with ever-increasing bad news.

You need to be strong to stand up to the emotional stress of conditioning.

Be sure, however, that you understand the difference between honest feedback and manipulative conditioning.

Conditioning stresses you, but with honest feedback, you will feel that the agent is working for you, not against you.

For example, if prospective buyers say that your home looks too cramped, the agent may suggest you declutter or consider 'staging' (see question 121).

One of the most frightening parts of conditioning is ridiculously low offers. For example, if you want $1 million for your home, agents may pass on offers as low as $700 000, even $650 000. Agents are legally required to pass on all buyer offers. But if they are giving you too many low offers, you need to ask why they are showing your home to buyers who can't afford it.

The best agents will always identify and qualify prospective buyers before showing your home. The term 'qualifying' is explained in question 162.

And when the best agents give you honest feedback — as opposed to manipulative conditioning — you won't feel miserable; you will feel hopeful, even uplifted.

With honest and positive feedback the best agents make you feel better.

# 6 What is meant by 'flipping' a property?

To 'flip' a property means to buy it for a low price and resell it for a much higher price, often immediately.

With flippers, agents often get two commissions. The first commission when they sell the property to the flipper below its value. And the second commission when they resell the property on behalf of the flipper for its true value.

The next question you may ask is, 'Isn't this unethical?' Sure, but the real estate industry is not renowned for its high standards of ethics.

# 7 How do I make sure my home is not flipped?

An older agent once dispensed some brutal advice to a younger agent: 'You don't get into real estate to make commission on sales. You get into real estate to find deals'.

'Deals'? Yes, underpriced property. So beware: everyone — from dodgy agents to property dealers to major developers — all of them are looking for a bargain.

Property gurus teach get-rich-quick students to search for the Four Ds: properties that involve Death, Divorce, Debt or Dummies. Dummies are defined as 'owners who don't realise how much their homes are worth'. Make sure you're not the 'dummy' these vultures feed on.

The best — and perhaps only — way to protect yourself from having your home bought cheaply and instantly resold is to know the true value of your home. And make sure you know this value before you hire an agent.

Ideally, to give yourself extra safety, you should hire a registered valuer — one independent of any agents you might consider. Unlike agents, valuers don't care what you think of the price they quote. You pay them for their professional advice — and their superior knowledge — which includes their opinion of its value.

Agents have a vested interest. Many will give you a false high quote to entice you to sign up. If they feel they are the only agent giving an appraisal, a dodgy agent may underquote so that they can sell your home to a flipper, an investor or a developer.

Probably the most heinous cases in real estate are those where agents take advantage of naïve elderly home sellers, some with dementia. That's another D consumers need to know. And don't say it doesn't happen. Offending agents rarely get caught.

# 8 What does 'Don't sign anything' mean?

For 25 years I have been repeating three words to consumers: *Don't sign anything!* I have said these words millions of times. Sometimes, people see me in the street and yell, 'Don't sign anything, mate'.

In 2002, I wrote a book call *Don't Sign Anything!* It was 400 pages telling consumers how to protect themselves in the real estate world.

I have had pencils, scratch pads, baseball caps, T-shirts, even umbrellas, emblazoned with the words *Don't sign anything*.

And still consumers get themselves into trouble by signing documents. They employ agents who undersell their property. They buy investment properties that are hundreds of thousands of dollars overpriced. Millions of consumers do tremendous damage to their financial lives. All because they sign documents.

Of course, to buy or sell real estate you must (at some stage) sign something. What I mean by 'Don't sign anything' is this: *Do not sign anything until you are sure you are safe.*

Or until you answer the question, 'What is the worst that can happen to me if I sign this document?' If most consumers answered that question, they would never sign so many documents — at least not without legal advice and/or deleting nasty clauses and conditions.

Your signature is the one thing over which you have complete control. And yet many major mistakes in life can be traced back to a signature.

Be careful. Real estate is known for bringing out the worst in people.

That's why I say *Don't sign anything*... until you are sure you are safe.

I also want to say another three words in addition to 'Don't sign anything!': *Don't pay anything* until your home is sold and you are happy with the price and the service.

---

## Key takeaways from part 1

- It is vital to understand the basics of how the real estate industry operates.
- Research shows that 95 per cent of people do not trust agents. This makes them the least trusted of all professions. The ethical standards have never been worse.
- The aim of all agents is to *list* homes for sale. Agents want sellers more than they want buyers.
- Honest agents often don't appear as the best agents because sellers don't like to hear the truth about the true value of their homes. Honest agents lose business to dishonest ones.

- Many sellers choose agents who inflate the likely selling price. This means that, many times, the biggest liar is selected as the listing agent.
- Agents will often attempt to persuade sellers to lower prices. Consider hiring a valuer before you contact an agent. Valuers will give you an unbiased and often more accurate estimate of your home's value.
- Beware of 'flippers'—that is, dealers who buy under value and then sell for true value.
- Remember these three words: *Don't sign anything!* Never sign until you're sure you're safe.
- Remember three more words: *Don't pay anything!* Don't pay until your home is sold and you're happy. Australian sellers are the most overcharged in the world.

# PART 2

# PLANNING TO SELL

The questions in this part will force you to think about what's in your best interests.

Three words frighten most salespeople: *Think about it*.

But that's exactly what you must do *before* you decide to sell. Make time to think it over. Look carefully at what lies ahead. Don't sign up with the first agent who tells you what you want to hear. Tell them that you want to think about it.

Salespeople are trained in how to overcome that feared objection. And the reason most salespeople don't want you to think about it is because if you do, you'll discover information that may cause you to reject their oh-so-sweet sales pitch.

Thinking might involve hard work. It might take time. But nothing is harder — or more disappointing — when selling your home than realising, after you have sold, that you could have obtained a better price. And saved thousands of dollars in expenses. It's far better to say, 'I am glad I did' than to say, 'I wish I had'.

You probably spent years of your life studying your profession so that you could earn a decent income and build your assets. So please spend a few hours (that's all) studying how to protect your greatest asset.

Abraham Lincoln famously said, 'If you give me six hours to chop down a tree, I will spend the first four hours sharpening my axe'.

Please read these next 21 questions — and their answers — carefully.

And please ... *think before you act.*

## Questions in this part

9. Do I really have to sell?
10. How much time should I devote to research?
11. When is the best time to sell a home?
12. What are the most common reasons for selling a home?
13. Should I reveal why I'm selling my home?
14. How long does it take to sell a home?
15. Should I be concerned about privacy issues?
16. Agents say my home is overcapitalised. What can I do?
17. Who can I trust for accurate statistics?
18. Who can I trust to give me accurate and objective support?
19. Should I take advice from friends?
20. What if a family member or friend wants to buy my home?
21. What does it cost to sell one home and buy another?
22. Should I sell first or buy first?
23. At what point am I legally obligated to sell?
24. What is the best result I can expect when selling?
25. What is the worst that can happen when selling?
26. Should I use a lawyer or a less costly conveyancer?
27. Should I get a building/pest report and offer it to prospective buyers?
28. Do I need a For Sale sign?
29. What are the worst mistakes made by most home sellers?

# 9 Do I really have to sell?

Selling a home — especially your family home — is one of the most stressful events in life. The longer you have lived in your home, the more stressful it is to sell it.

So, do you want to sell? I mean, *really want* to sell?

Are you going to be better off having sold your home than if you kept your home? By 'better off', I don't mean financially; I mean *happily*.

If not, why are you selling?

Perhaps you are selling because of forces outside your control. Such as financial problems, health issues or, perhaps the most heart-breaking of all, because your home is now too much for you. As you age, you are no longer capable of maintaining your home without assistance. And, these days, the cost of assistance — from a handyman to an electrician — is beyond the reach of many elderly folk.

But please wait. Pause.

If you don't want to sell, why not try and find a way to keep your home? Especially if you are elderly. The move from a beloved family home in a familiar neighbourhood to a retirement home (or worse, a nursing home) can be traumatic for some elderly people. It's akin to an established tree being uprooted and planted elsewhere. Many soon die.

## *Try before you sell*

When I was an agent, I often went to homes filled with sadness. People were selling due to sudden trauma: illness, divorce, bankruptcy, business failure, family disputes … the list was endless. Many times, I would try and find an alternative to selling. I wanted people to keep their home. I never felt comfortable profiting from misery.

One of the most common errors was made by recent retirees who planned to sell in Sydney and move to a favoured destination, often to Queensland's Gold Coast.

Moving house is more expensive than most homeowners realise. It can also be risky, especially if you move to an unfamiliar area. If you have regularly visited an area on holidays and fallen in love with it, it doesn't mean you should live there.

So often, I would see newly retired couples sell up quickly, move up the coast and, within months — even weeks — ask themselves, 'What have we done?' While their newly chosen area may have seemed alluringly beautiful, there is one thing missing from all newly chosen areas: your 'circle'.

When you move far away from a home where you've lived happily for years, you may not immediately realise what you've left behind — nor how emotionally valuable it is to you.

Your circle includes your family (especially grandchildren) and, of course, close friends. When you leave your nest of many years, it can feel like you've abandoned those you love. And even though your new area may have many good people, few will match your circle back home. Indeed, if you move to a new area and use the expression 'back home' too often it means that your body may have relocated but your heart is back where you left it.

Aside from realising that you ache for your circle, you will then face the additional cost of selling up and moving back to where you felt at home. You may suffer a significant financial loss on the newly bought home. And, even if homes back in the city have not risen in price, it will still cost you a packet to buy back into your former area.

So, what to do?

Simple. Rather than sell up and buy a home in the area you think you love, you should rent out your family home, move to your new area and rent a home there. Within a few months, a year at the most, you'll know if you've made the right decision. If yes, then sell your home back in the city and buy in your new area.

If you are not happy, go home. Back to where you belong.

As an agent, when I gave this advice to elderly people, they would smile with delight at such a simple, safe and pragmatic approach.

But then they (usually the businessperson of the pair) would often ask me, 'What do you get out of talking us *out* of selling?'

My reply was always the same: 'I promised, when I opened my real estate office, that I would put the interests of my clients ahead of my own interests. If I know how to remove your risk of selling and regretting it and then being locked out of the city market, I am not going to conceal that solution from you because it's against my commercial interests'.

Sure, I may not have got a commission — not then and there. But if or when they did decide to sell, there was only one agent they were going to choose: Jenman.

Plus, I soon noticed an unexpected positive side-effect to my philosophy of always putting the interests of homeowners ahead of my financial interests: a stream of recommendations. Many other sellers would contact me as word spread that I was an agent who could be trusted.

# 10 How much time should I devote to research?

How would you like to earn $1000 per hour?

And that's conservative.

The true value in carrying out research before selling a home can easily amount to $5000 an hour. My hope is that you will save thousands of dollars or learn how to sell your home for tens (maybe hundreds) of thousands of dollars more after reading this book.

There is a tragic irony in the lives of many hard-working people. They spend years learning a profession to earn a high income. But then most don't spend hours learning how to make sure their most valuable asset sells for the highest market price. Don't make that mistake. Spend time doing some due diligence.

# 11 When is the best time to sell a home?

There are several arguments about when is the best time to sell a home. For example, spring is when most people think it's best to sell. But in spring there are often more houses for sale, which means more competition, so it can be better for buyers than sellers.

A shortage of stock drives prices up. This argument states that you should sell when agents are short of listings, which is often in winter.

The type of property you own can affect when you sell. For example, if you owned a farm, you wouldn't sell in a drought. You'd wait for the rainy season when there is an abundance of grass.

If your home has a pool, the best time to sell may be during a heatwave when children are frolicking in the water. Imagine if your friends were having a barbeque around the pool at the same time. And imagine again that your home was beautifully air conditioned. Almost irresistible.

But when winter comes and the pool cleaner hasn't been around — and the water is green and full of rotting leaves — buyers will be put off. They'll think of maintenance. Not the best time to sell.

If your home has an open fireplace and you live in a cool city, picture how inviting your home will feel in winter: at dusk may be the perfect time. A crackling fire can melt the coldest heart.

So, you need to ask, 'When is the best time to sell *my* home?' The answer is, 'Whenever your home is looking its best and when there is, hopefully, a big demand for homes like yours'.

Think of the best attributes of your home. If it has a stunning view at sunset, surely this will appeal to buyers. Ask, 'What made me fall

in love with my home? What appealed to me most when I first saw it?'
Try to duplicate the same conditions that prompted you to buy your
home, and you might find buyers feel the same way as you once did.
Even more so.

Good homes are not like people. Even movie stars don't look as
good as they did once they age. But many homes improve with age,
especially if they have been loved and well maintained.

Be sure of one thing, however: it's impossible to pick the top of a
market when selling, just as it's impossible to pick the bottom when
buying. If you sell and re-buy in the same market, you should be
unaffected.

But always consider the most important factor of all: as long as
you're happy, you've made the right decision.

# 12 What are the most common reasons for selling a home?

There are three main reasons why homeowners sell homes.

## 1 Upgraders

Sellers in this class can range from former first home buyers now
looking to climb another rung on the real estate ladder, through to
those who've done well in life and want to buy a gorgeous home. Or
perhaps they are moving from a small home in a city to rolling acres
in the country. Upgrading has many different meanings.

## 2 Downsizers

Downsizing does not necessarily mean downgrading. A common
reason for downsizing is when a large family becomes a two-person
family, such as when children have left home. Or when elderly folk

want to move to a retirement home — or more substantive care. A fortunate few move in with family.

### 3 Liquidators

Liquidating does not necessarily mean an owner is in financial trouble. There are many reasons owners may need cash: to start a business; to assist relatives (often children); to reduce debt; to travel; to splurge on luxury goods; or to dissolve a personal or business partnership. And, sadly, deceased estates come under this category too.

# 13 Should I reveal why I'm selling my home?

It depends. If revealing your reason for selling may hurt your chances of achieving the best price, then no, don't reveal your reason for selling.

For example, if you are in financial trouble or suffering ill health. The real estate world can be heartless. Some agents promote sellers' distress. They use words like 'forced sale', which creates the impression that you can be forced down in price.

The mere fact of selling a home can give rise to suspicion in the minds of buyers. Therefore, rather than using terms with negative connotations like 'must sell', use the expression 'reluctant sale'. It's more positive. Especially if you have lived in (and loved) your home for many years.

And if ever you get the direct question, 'Why are you selling?' and you don't feel comfortable revealing your reason, simply reply, 'We are relocating'.

It's important, however, to make it clear that you are a *serious* seller — not one of those sellers who asks a crazy price (and 'will only sell if we get it') as if they are trying to win the lottery by finding someone rich enough (or silly enough) to overpay for their home.

If you have a nice home — or a home with potential — and it will appeal to many potential buyers, the best way to get the best price is to be fair in all you do. Set a good asking price, choose a good agent, keep control and you'll be assured of a good result.

# 14 How long does it take to sell a home?

Australia's homes are among the fastest selling in the world. The average time from listing a home to an unconditional sale is about 30 days. In the United States, it takes twice as long at 60 days. In the UK, it takes about six months to sell a home.

Surveys show that when agents sell their own homes, however, they usually take longer to sell. And often sell for a better price. This is because agents are willing to wait for the best buyer. However, when they are selling other people's homes, they often push sellers to accept the first serious offer knowing that this will give them their commission sooner.

But what is the 'average' time it takes? Many factors affect the time it takes to sell. Everything from the area, to the condition of the home, to the competency of the agent and finally to the price asked for the home. All these factors affect time.

It's often said that you can pick a time, or you can pick a price. It's hard to pick both. If you want a quick sale you may have to accept a lower price. If you hold out for a high price, it may take longer. However, if you have a beautiful home in a tightly held area (that is, an area where homes do not come up for sale very often) and you sell during a boom, you may get a high price in a short time. Such instances are the exception though, not the norm.

So, decide what suits you and plan accordingly. But don't be too stubborn and hold out too long. If you start too high, you'll increase your chances of taking too long and selling too low.

# 15 Should I be concerned about privacy issues?

If you are doing anything in the real estate world — from selling, to buying, to leasing — you should be concerned about privacy. Not only for your personal safety but also for your financial safety.

Unlike the medical or legal profession — indeed, unlike most personal situations today — privacy in real estate is almost nonexistent.

Most people can discover personal and property details about anyone. Even being famous won't help you. It is often easier to find information on celebrities than ordinary citizens.

Without wanting to reveal exactly how it's done, here are a few examples of what *is* done — with some suggestions on how you can increase your personal privacy and safety.

## Agents will talk

If consumers heard how some agents talk about them, they'd be horrified. Not just in disparaging terms — which is bad enough — but in revealing confidential information.

Most times, revealing personal information works against the interests of consumers. That's one of the reasons so many agents reveal private details. It helps them make sales.

Check it out for yourself. Some agents are so contemptuous of their clients' privacy, they'll reveal the most private information to the most anonymous people.

Just visit any open-for-inspection and whisper to the agent a question such as, 'So, what's the story with this place, mate?' Out will come all the family secrets — everything from health to tragedy to financial matters.

If your home is for sale, try having a friend pose as a buyer. And brace yourself for when your friend reports back to you.

Many agents don't care about your privacy. Make it known to your agent that your privacy is important. Of course, most will say they respect their clients' confidences. Make it clear that you will have friends mystery-shop the agent to be sure your confidences are kept. (See question 34 for information on mystery-shopping.) There is no need to threaten them. Just stress how much you value your privacy.

## Beware of online advertising

The most brazen breaches of privacy occur with millions of family homes in Australia because you can go online and look through their homes.

Even when a home is sold, website owners seldom remove property details. This causes enormous distress to buyers who value their privacy. Some buyers (now owners) plead for months with agents and web owners to have personal information removed. All to no avail.

Almost no-one seems to care.

### Treasure your privacy

I have heard of at least one instance where a killer entered a home and murdered a young lady. The home's floor plan was online. He went straight to her bedroom. How many other cases — in this age of stalking and domestic violence — occur all over the country?

Just ask any police officer if it's a good idea to show the world photographs of the interior of your home with a floorplan of that interior.

Or an online video where an agent says, 'Let me show you through this lovely home'.

Show who?! What are you doing? Don't you care about your clients' rights to privacy?

How much publicity are you getting for yourself, agent? How many leads are you getting at the expense of trusting sellers? And most despicable of all, how much are (some) videographers paying you for each video?

Despite what agents and advertisers tell you, it is *not* necessary to have lots of details of your home online.

Indeed, personal information is disconcerting to people who value privacy.

Who wants to buy a home that anyone can see the inside of for years to come? Who wants to live in a home that thousands of lookers have wandered through online?

Sellers, you don't know how much damage you do to yourselves by putting so much information online. The purpose of advertising is not to *sell* your property, it's to create an enquiry from a genuine buyer.

It is then the agent's job to *identify* and *qualify* prospective buyers — before giving them details of your property.

## Protecting your online privacy

I recommend not allowing anyone — other than identified and qualified buyers — to see the interior of your home. (See question 162 for an explanation on qualifying.) Why let millions of people view your personal details when, in reality, all you need is one buyer? Use basic advertising, if you must, but reveal your personal details only when it's safe to do so.

Ideally, of course, you should find an agent who uses advertising as a last resort. A hard-working, smart agent. They do exist.

Most agents have hundreds of buyers on file. But they are too lazy to call buyers. They'd rather splash your private details all over the internet, thereby promoting themselves and getting extra leads at your expense while risking your safety.

And wilfully damaging the value of your home.

Many sellers don't realise that if they advertise their home and it hasn't sold in a few weeks, the value drops. Buyers wonder what's wrong with it. Why hasn't it sold? Oh, that's right, it must be too dear. That's why it's rejected. Meanwhile, the website companies rake in billions of dollars, and the agents get free publicity and plenty of new leads.

Don't let it happen to you. If an agent doesn't know how to find buyers without breaching your privacy, find a better agent.

## Nothing is private anymore

With the decline in landlines and the rise in mobile phones, it was getting harder for agents to contact people. But not anymore. Now there are several services designed for agents to access millions of people.

Got a silent number or a private address? It doesn't matter — they'll track you down. There are plenty of online advertisements that talk about how information is power. They offer a 360-degree view of both the property and the owners, boasting what this information can do for you. They tell you everything you need to know: when the property was last on the market, when it was withdrawn, where the owners can be contacted, what their details are ...

Plus, drivers licences, dates of birth, your partner's details ... you name it. Maybe even your blood group. Surely not.

All for around $150 a month and reportedly with more than 10 000 real estate agents gladly paying for it. It's a real estate stalking stampede and it's coming your way.

Yes, millions of dollars are being earned by creators of these systems who, despite furious accusations, claim it's perfectly legal.

Perhaps, but it's certainly Orwellian in its creepiness.

### Avoiding unsolicited phone calls

Set your phone to total silence other than for your loved ones. Record a voice mail message asking callers to text before you will consider replying.

Or get a second phone — one for loved ones only. Protect this number with your life. After all, your private life does depend on it.

# 16 Agents say my home is overcapitalised. What can I do?

Just because your home is overcapitalised, it does not have to be undersold.

Let's define 'overcapitalise'. To overcapitalise means to spend more money on the home — building, renovating or improving — than the home may then be worth.

For example, let's say you buy a house for $1.5 million, the median price for an area. You spend $1 million renovating it. Technically it now 'owes' you $2.5 million.

But even years later, local agents may say that you will be unlikely to get more than the median price for your area. And that's currently $2 million.

Therefore, according to the local agents, you're facing a capital loss of half a million dollars.

It doesn't matter who you are, losing money is never pleasant. Indeed, losing $500 000 can feel financially nauseating.

So, what can you do?

The first thing you need is a positive agent, one who is prepared to work hard and will try to sell your home for the amount it owes you — or more.

Please understand that typical agents are not interested in getting a high sale price — especially if it means working hard. They want a sale, but at any price.

You need an agent who will make a supreme effort to recover the total amount — perhaps more — than the home owes you. It is often said that 'selling is the transference of enthusiasm'. If your agent is not enthusiastic about your home, the buyers are unlikely to be enthusiastic. Some agents are so incompetent they'll tell the buyers that your home is overcapitalised.

You should reject agents who expect you to lose money. Regardless of whether they can justify their opinion, it is near criminal not to try to sell your home for what it owes you.

So, the first rule when selling an overcapitalised home is to find an overenthusiastic agent.

The second is to find an agent who appreciates what it has cost you to improve your home, and what benefits the new owners can enjoy. If buyers fall in love with your home and they can afford it, they will buy it — overcapitalised or not.

# 17 Who can I trust for accurate statistics?

Louis Christopher from SQM Research.

Mr Christopher is the most honest, the most accurate and the most decent property analyst in Australia. Many years ago, he lost his job as a statistician for a major media company when he steadfastly refused to release fake figures to benefit agents.

Following his unjust dismissal — and while his world seemed to be coming apart — Louis Christopher started his own research business. Today, SQM Research employs 25 staff and has over 2000 clients with a revenue of over $7 million.

# 18 Who can I trust to give me accurate and objective support?

There is no better 'payment' in my life than being trusted by people I like — especially homeowners of Australia. So, of course, I hope you feel you can trust me. I always strive to do right, and I always put the best interests of real estate consumers first.

When I first heard this question, the names of several agents came to mind; however, things often change in real estate. In the past I have had many agents I trusted for years breach my trust. Some agents find it near impossible to resist what's known as the 'dark side'.

For example, an agent in Sydney's eastern suburbs who always had a 'pay on success' policy suddenly changed his policy. At the direct behest of his franchise bosses, he was now forced to charge all sellers huge and usually needless marketing expenses.

But then, after a long conversation, he conceded the following: 'Neil, when you recommend us to sellers, I will treat them ethically and not force them to pay needless costs'.

I thanked him.

As the call ended, I asked, 'Why don't you treat all your sellers ethically by offering them all a "no sale no charge" policy?'

His answer was sad and simple: 'Head office will not allow it'.

If you wish to know which agents I currently believe you can trust, I hope you contact my vendor advocacy service, Jenman Support. Sure, Jenman Support are paid a support fee by agents. But we never charge home sellers for our support or help. Nor do we ask sellers to sign anything.

Our major goal is protecting the interests of home sellers and supporting them so that they get the best result when they sell. If they don't sell, they are never out of pocket for needless expenses.

This is the service that we urge all agents to offer because it instantly identifies agents who can be trusted.

# 19 Should I take advice from friends?

These days, everyone seems to be an expert in real estate. No matter what their profession, scores of armchair experts hand out real estate advice.

Spending hours trawling websites, visiting open homes or attending auctions does not make someone a real estate expert. There is a huge difference between a pseudo expert and a real expert. Pseudo experts — and sadly this may include friends, even family — can be dangerous advisors. It is often said that one of the worst things you can say about another person is that they 'mean well'. Meaning well is different from *doing* well.

Sure, listen to your friends. But remember, real estate propaganda is seductive. So often, a well-meaning person giving advice is regurgitating real estate sophistry. And this means playing straight into the hands of dodgy agents.

If people don't do their own research and if they don't understand the intricacies and shenanigans in the real estate industry, they're not qualified to give advice to anyone. And 'qualified' doesn't mean having a real estate licence. It means being able to give advice that's in the best interests of the person to whom the advice is given.

Be careful. And, if a 'friend' seems to be pushing too hard for you to use a certain agency, maybe they are being paid by that agency. To recommend any company or person based purely on financial reward is about as bad as it gets.

As many rogues know, 'You can't cheat your enemies; they don't trust you. But your friends are easy to cheat'.

# 20 What if a family member or friend wants to buy my home?

If you sign an Exclusive Listing Agreement you are excluded from selling your home to any person without paying full commission to the agent. The agent has complete control over the sale of your home during the time period of the Listing Agreement — and often until you cancel the agreement in writing. Whoever buys it — under any conditions — the agent still gets paid.

However, if you sign a Sole Agency Agreement, you should be able to sell to a family member or a friend without any cost or further obligation to the agent.

Of course, if the agent has impressed you with their effort thus far, you may decide to remunerate them in some way. Do whatever you feel is fair.

With a Sole Agency Agreement you, not the agent, are in control.

# 21 What does it cost to sell one home and buy another?

Experience has likely taught you that things always cost more than you expect. And your income — especially from the sale of a large item like a house (or a car) — is often less than you expect.

Therefore, it's always best to overestimate your expenses and underestimate your income. While, at first, this may seem frightening, the end result is that you should end up better off than you expected.

So, here's how you estimate costs when you sell one home and buy another...

Allow for the *total* costs to be 10 per cent of the price of the property you are buying.

So, for example, if you are selling a home for $1.5 million and you are buying another home for $2 million, your total costs will be (an absolute maximum of) $200 000.

That's the amount you should allow based on the overestimate/ underestimate principle.

# 22 Should I sell first or buy first?

Either choice — selling first or buying first — can land you in trouble, both financially and emotionally. If you sell first and can't find a home to buy, you'll be out in the street (as it seems).

If you buy first and then can't easily sell your current home, you'll be under pressure to slash the price. Or you'll be paying thousands of dollars in interest for a bridging loan.

When you are in a hurry to sell, you are at the mercy of bargain hunters. Especially if your agent promotes your home with words such as 'Bought elsewhere. Must sell'.

The solution — although some agents don't like it (because it takes longer to get commission) — is simple and obvious.

It's this: *Buy and sell at the same time.*

Don't think it's too complicated. Ignore what some agents say. They want their commission as soon as possible. If this means more stress on you to sell cheaply or if you risk being homeless, so what. They want their commission.

But when you do what's in your best interests — namely, sell and buy at the same time (it's called a 'simultaneous settlement') — the agent must wait for their commission.

So, what's more important to you: your best interests or the agent's best interests?

And remember two things: it's perfectly legal (check with your lawyer or conveyancer) and it's oh-so-simple. There is one word to remember. One word that makes it possible for you to sell your home at the same time as you buy another.

That word is 'terms'. (Or perhaps 'conditions'.)

You can sell your home under any terms you choose. If you want to make the sale of your home subject to the Western Bulldogs making the eight in the next AFL season, you can do so.

Conversely, you can buy a home under any terms you choose. As can all buyers. If someone wants to buy your home, they can make the sale subject to Collingwood making the final eight next season.

Most sellers and buyers — influenced by most agents — only focus on one factor when they sell or buy real estate: *price.*

But the terms can have as much, even more, of an influence on the sale as the price. Indeed, many sales would never happen if one side (either buyer or seller) did not agree to terms requested by the other side. Note the word 'requested', not 'demanded'. Courtesy and consideration will lead to a more successfully negotiated sale.

Here are three simple steps to selling and buying simultaneously:

1.  Place your home for sale on the condition that you will not legally commit to sell until you find a home to buy.
2.  Search for another home. When you find a home you like, make your purchase conditional upon the satisfactory sale of your current home. Such an arrangement is common. It's known as a 'subject to' sale.
3.  When you have found a buyer for your current home you are then ready to sell and buy simultaneously.

Make sure, of course, that during the entire transaction you stay in close contact with your legal advisor.

# 23 At what point am I legally obligated to sell?

Generally, you cannot be forced to sell your home unless you enter into a legally binding contract or document that commits you to sell.

The scary word in the above paragraph is 'generally'.

Evil can be seductive. In the real estate world, some evil characters prey on decent (and too trusting) homeowners. For example, a lovely couple offer to buy your home. They pay you a small deposit ($500 cash) as a show of good faith. They ask you for a receipt, which seems reasonable. You sign the receipt. (*Don't sign anything!*) What is written on that receipt could legally obligate you to sell your home below its value.

If you think these words are written to scare you, that's right.

It is essential to get independent legal advice before signing any documents. Even if you sign an agent's Listing Agreement without reading the fine print you could be forced to sell your home or pay the agent for not selling your home.

This may sound complicated but that's why you must check the fine print — even if it needs a magnifying glass.

And get a legal opinion.

# 24 What is the best result I can expect when selling?

A dreadful irony in real estate is that thousands of sellers think they got a great result — and walk away happy — without knowing they could have obtained a much better price.

The best result when selling your home is to get *the highest possible price with the least possible stress*. And to pay a fair rate of commission (and costs).

If this seems too good to be true, that's because many agents never achieve such a result. Don't let what typically happens, however, happen to you.

Put the effort into finding the right agent who can get you a high price with low stress.

# 25 What is the worst that can happen when selling?

The biggest disasters that befall sellers are mostly caused by hiring the wrong agent.

If, for whatever reason, you *don't* sell your home, the worst that can happen (immediately) is that you will be thousands of dollars out of pocket for needless marketing costs. You may also discover that the value of your home has been damaged by too much exposure and too much negative word of mouth.

If you do sell your home, the worst that can happen is that you discover — after you sell — that you sold below the best market price. Your home may have been bought by a dealer, and you soon see it back on the market — with minor or no improvements — at a price well above the price at which you sold it.

Disasters such as this are caused by hiring an incompetent or dishonest agent.

So, the most important question you should ask (and answer) when entering the real estate world is, 'What is the worst that can happen?'

Let me answer that with a short story.

## Sadly, there are some things you can't predict

Colin and Marsha were in their 70s. They decided to sell their home in Sydney's Hills. Marsha wanted to be closer to their grandchildren. Colin was happy to stay in the Hills but he acceded to Marsha's wishes. Soon after they signed contracts to sell — and before settlement — Marsha died. Although heartbroken after 52 years together, Colin no longer wished to sell. There is a clause in most sale contracts that says if either party dies or becomes mentally incapacitated, the sale can be rescinded. Incredibly, the conveyancer omitted the dying component of the clause. The buyers pushed Colin to sell. Fortunately, he got external help, cancelled the sale and kept his home.

# 26 Should I use a lawyer or a less costly conveyancer?

I always use a lawyer for real estate matters.

These days, however, conveyancing companies are more competent and trustworthy than in the 1980s. Many such companies employ lawyers or are managed/owned by lawyers. If you can save money and have the same legal protection with a conveyancing company as a legal firm, then, of course, a less expensive conveyancer is worth considering.

# 27 Should I get a building/pest report and offer it to prospective buyers?

Yes. Definitely.

There is no legal need for you to provide inspection reports on your home. Disclosure laws in Australia (except the ACT) are below minimum requirements in other countries.

But why should the law — in our business or personal lives — be our minimum standard?

It's expensive to sell a house. It's also expensive to buy one. A building and pest report can cost up to $1000. Some buyers waste many thousands of dollars buying reports on multiple properties. Often, buyers are misled by agents about the likely sale price of a property. As a result, they fork out money on reports for a home they never had a chance of buying.

Therefore, anything you can do to make life easier for buyers will make your home more appealing. The eventual buyer for your home will be so pleased with your upfront disclosure, they may reimburse you the cost of the building report — especially if you guarantee its veracity.

Do all you can to disclose everything about your property — faults as well as benefits. If you hide faults, buyers will likely find them.

Causing distrust in a negotiation is not conducive to achieving the best result.

# 28 Do I need a For Sale sign?

Yes.

A For Sale sign is your most effective and least expensive form of advertising. The best prospects for your home are those familiar with your neighbourhood. They live in the area. Or they have family or friends in the area. And, if your area is what's known as a tightly held area, you will likely get a better price from locals.

Some people — especially migrants — are keen to live near relatives. These people will often pay well above market value to buy a home near a family member. Imagine if you refuse to have a For Sale sign and your home gets quietly sold to out-of-town strangers. As you go next door to say goodbye, your neighbours are not just sad that you're leaving, they're devastated that they didn't know you were selling.

The main reason that sellers will not allow a For Sale sign to be put up is because they don't want neighbours to know they are selling. But locals are the people most likely to pay the highest price.

### The importance of a For Sale sign

A story from Mosman shows what often happens. An agent convinced the sellers to spend $50 000 on marketing costs. The buyer came from the For Sale sign. It was their neighbour.

If you are a genuine home seller, a For Sale sign is essential for giving you the best chance of getting the best result. And no, despite what an agent may tell you, the sign only needs two words (For Sale) and one phone number.

> *Remember, the purpose of advertising is to* attract, *not to sell.*

# 29 What are the worst mistakes made by most home sellers?

Myriad mistakes are made by home sellers; most are outlined in this book.

Seven of the most serious mistakes, however, are the below:

1. Selling by public auction (instead of private negotiation or silent auction)
2. Damaging the value of your home by allowing thousands of lookers to view it online
3. Being persuaded to spend thousands of dollars on needless advertising
4. Declining to insist on a guarantee from an agent so that you are not 'locked in'
5. Not making agents work for their commission by making personal contact with buyers already known to them before risking the cost and damage of advertising
6. Not taking the time to find the right agent
7. Dropping the price instead of dropping the agent.

## Key takeaways from part 2

▸ Selling a home is highly stressful. For the elderly it's often traumatic.

▸ Selling a home and re-buying another home is enormously expensive.

▸ If you sell your home, will you be happier? If not, why sell? Seek an alternative.

▸ If you plan to relocate far away, consider renting out your home, not selling. Then rent a home in the new area. Wait a year. If you're happy, *then* sell and re-buy.

▸ The best time to sell is when your home is looking its best *and* it's in high demand.

▸ Be wary of revealing your reason for selling. Just say you are 'relocating'.

▸ Always remember: selling is the transference of enthusiasm.

▸ On average, it takes about 30 days to find a buyer for your home.

▸ Your privacy is paramount. Do not reveal much personal information publicly.

▸ Friends might be well-meaning, but they can give the wrong advice.

▸ Understand the difference between an Exclusive Agency and a Sole Agency.

▸ If you are selling and re-buying, allow 10 per cent of the price of the property you will be buying as a safe overestimate of your total costs.

▸ Sell first or buy first? You can do both together. It's called a 'simultaneous settlement'.

*(continued)*

- ▸ Get independent legal advice before you sign, no matter how safe things seem. Always obey this rule. Your signature is one thing over which you have total control.
- ▸ The biggest mistake made by sellers is hiring the wrong agent. (More tips in part 3.)
- ▸ Consider getting a building and pest report and offering it to buyers.
- ▸ A For Sale sign is essential. It often attracts the best-paying buyers.
- ▸ Be aware of the seven worst mistakes made by home sellers.

# PART 3

# HIRING AN AGENT

In this part you will learn how to recognise the best agents: the ones with the skill to get you the best price and the integrity not to overcharge you or, worse, leave you thousands of dollars out of pocket without selling your home.

Nothing is more important than finding a great agent to sell your home. The biggest expense for most home sellers is choosing the wrong agent.

The following questions and answers will reveal the different types of agents, how to choose the best agent to sell your home and, finally, how to work successfully with the agent you hire.

The best advice about finding the best agent is to be firm. Keep going until you find the right agent. It cannot be said too often: better to spend three or four weeks searching for the right agent than to spend three or four months stuck with the wrong agent.

These questions in part 3 will show you how to find an agent who will be a reliable partner for you in the selling process.

# Questions in this part

58. If other agents offer to match their competitors, should I consider using them?
59. If I sign up with an experienced agent, will I be delegated to a junior?
60. Can I list with more than one agent?
61. What can happen after I sign an agent's Listing Agreement?
62. If negotiation skills are so important, why do so few agents learn these skills?
63. How can I design a smart and effective plan to sell my home?
64. Do agents have a plan to sell my home?
65. Should I let my agent enlist the help of other agents?
66. What happens if I accidentally sign up with the wrong agent?
67. Is 'introducing' a buyer the same as 'selling' my home?
68. Why do agents 'knock' other agents?

# 30 Do I have to use an agent to sell my home?

One of the myths in the real estate industry is that sellers get a better deal if they use an agent than if they go it alone. This is nonsense. The opposite is often true. Sellers who reject typical agents can get a far better result: fewer costs and a higher sale price.

> *As you will see throughout this book, many agents do nothing that most sellers could not do for themselves.*

Incredibly, some homeowners think they must use a real estate agent (by law) to sell their home. The truth is you can use your mate next door to help you sell your home (provided your mate doesn't receive money on your behalf). Indeed, you and your mate would surely do a better job than some agents. After all, mates care about each other.

Consider what many agents typically do — not what they say they will do but what they actually do. Agents don't sell homes. That's another myth. Buyers buy homes. The 'sell' in real estate is convincing sellers that they need a real estate agent.

As a seller, all you need is basic research and a legal representative to assist you with the title transfers. When you discover what many agents do, you will likely have two thoughts: first, 'Is that all they do?' and second, 'I could do that'.

You're right. Of course you could do what many agents do: place an ad online and wait for a buyer to show up.

Who knows your home better than you do? Which agent knows your street and those who live in the area better than you do?

So why pay tens of thousands of dollars in commission, thousands of dollars in needless marketing costs and, the costliest of all, undersell your home — often by hundreds of thousands of dollars?

The only time you should employ an agent is if you find a skilled agent who can achieve a fair price, who charges low marketing costs and whose commission can be justified.

One of the best ways to recognise competent (and ethical) agents is by looking for ones who offer a 'pay-only-on-success' method. These are agents who have such faith in their ability, they guarantee themselves.

Granted, agents who offer a guarantee are rare. But it's worth spending time looking for one.

If you can't find a skilled agent, you only have two choices: use a typical agent or do it yourself (to pay less and get a better price).

# 31 How important is my choice of agent?

It is incredibly important to choose a competent agent to sell your home. Many agents undersell homes. Their focus is on getting a sale — at any price.

The right agent can mean tens of thousands of extra dollars. It's easy to think that agents are identical. But that's incorrect. There are two types of agent: skilled agents and typical agents (more on the latter in question 32).

The typical agents use the typical systems that infect the industry. Same spiel, different faces.

If you must choose a *typical* agent, choose the one with the lowest commission because they're all the same. Typical agents do less, so pay them less.

But it's much better for you financially to spend time searching for a competent agent — even if you go outside your immediate area.

It cannot be overstated: the best agents get the best prices. So, if price is important to you, find the best agent.

Also, it's a good idea not to interview too many agents (at least not in person). The more agents who see your home, the more resentment you will create among the agents you don't choose. Agents don't like to miss out on listings. As most buyers circulate among most agents in the area where they are looking to buy, you don't want to create a dozen enemies. So, try not to call in 13 agents. You can only select one, so hopefully you can find the right one by researching (or mystery-shopping, which is explained in question 34) agents and then narrowing down your list to two or three agents.

For questions to ask agents that you interview, see question 46.

# 32 What is meant by the term 'a typical agent'?

Australia is one of the most expensive countries in the world in which to sell a home. This is due to the voracious greed of many agents. On top of the commission are billions (yes, billions!) of dollars in needless advertising costs. Plus, we have a continual litany of new and ever-increasing charges — as many as naïve sellers can be persuaded to pay.

Australia's total real estate market is worth around $11 trillion. In comparison, the stock market is worth around $1.5 trillion. If typical stockbrokers were doing the same as some real estate agents, the stockbrokers would face criminal charges.

Typical agents are dreadful negotiators. Therefore, most homes are undersold. Often by upwards of 10 per cent of the value. That's $100 000 lost for every million dollars.

Many agents (at least 85 per cent) could be classed as 'typical agents'. They use the typical flawed systems that infect the real estate world.

There are four main ways to recognise typical agents, most of whom are clones of one another.

1. *They lock you in.* They sign you up to an Exclusive Listing Agreement that's filled with clauses that benefit agents and harm sellers. They lock you in and have complete control over you and your home for three to six months. No matter what happens, if your home is sold, the agent gets paid. Should your home not be sold, you will likely lose thousands of dollars due to the second way of recognising typical agents.

2. *They expect you to pay up no matter what.* Typical agents demand that you pay thousands of dollars for 'marketing expenses' upfront (or to agree to pay later whether your home is sold or not). The main purpose of these expenses is to promote your agent. They call it 'raising their profile' (at your expense). Typical agents also use your money to find new leads. If your home doesn't sell, you lose thousands of dollars. It's 'heads they win; tails you lose'.

3. *Typical agents are lazy.* They rarely follow up buyers. They rarely even qualify buyers. (Question 162 explains the process of qualifying buyers.) They will open your home for 30 minutes a week and hope a buyer turns up who loves it, in which case the agent will make about $20 000 for every $1 000 000 value of the house. Remember this: the typical agent is doing nothing you couldn't do yourself. In fact, you could likely do better.

4. *They adopt the wrong selling method.* Typical agents use whatever selling method gets them their commission the fastest (such as by auction). Your goal is to sell your home for a good price. But the typical agent's goal is to sell your home for *any* price as soon as possible.

# 33 Is there evidence that some agents get higher prices?

Yes, there is evidence of some agents getting better prices for similar (or identical) properties in the same area. In 2018, a survey was conducted among agents in a Victorian regional centre. Buyers who had recently purchased homes were asked a series of questions, including the main one: 'Would you have paid more for this home than you did pay?'

In 90 per cent of cases, buyers admitted that they would have paid more. When asked why they didn't pay more, most said, 'We didn't have to'. They did what most buyers do: made an offer below the price they were willing to pay. In some cases, they were asked to increase their offers. But in most cases, they bought the home below their maximum offer.

Different agents had vastly different levels of negotiation competency. Some achieved the highest price in as many as half their sales. With one agency, however, every buyer (100 per cent) agreed that they would have paid more. This agency was underselling all the properties it sold.

There was only one agency with a perfect negotiation score. All buyers said they had paid the highest they were willing to pay. Ironically, this was the only agency that always used the buyers' price declaration (see question 173) on every sale.

*Note:* At the time of writing, research is being conducted in other areas. Early results are showing similar figures.

# 34 Should I mystery-shop agents? If so, how and when?

There are two times to mystery-shop agents. The first is to help you find the best agent to sell your home. The second is to check up on your chosen agent when your home is for sale.

Many agents treat buyers appallingly. They don't return phone calls. They don't follow up. And they have scant regard for the buyers' needs. The proof — aside from the massive amount of anecdotal evidence — that so many agents show complete disdain to buyers is this: all buyers eventually become sellers. And when they decide to sell, less than 20 per cent of former buyers list with the agent from whom they bought their home.

As a home seller, you need an agent who is respectful towards buyers, who qualifies them politely and who follows them up regularly. (See question 162 to understand how qualifying buyers works.)

To discover how agents treat buyers, contact a few agents and enquire about some homes they have for sale. If the agents don't call you back promptly, if they treat you disrespectfully or, worse, if they ignore you completely, this is not the agent you should choose to sell your home. Keep searching until you find an agent who treats buyers well.

The agents who treat buyers the best are the agents who get the best price.

The second time you should mystery-shop agents is when you become a seller. Have a friend contact your agent to ask questions about your home and then give you feedback. If you allow free-for-all open inspections on your home, send a friend to inspect your home and report on the conduct of the agent.

Be prepared to be shocked about how that friendly agent with whom you listed your home may now talk about you and your home.

If you are not happy with how the agent is conducting the sale of your home, you can dismiss the agent *provided that* you insisted on the right to do so at the time you listed your property. If you do not have the right to dismiss the agent, then you are stuck with them even if you don't like or respect them. You will most likely not be able to dismiss the agent until the expiry date of the Listing Agreement.

## 35 Do any agents offer guarantees?

Yes, some agents — usually the best (or occasionally, the desperate) — do offer a guarantee.

The three most important guarantees are:

1. *a dismissal guarantee.* If you are not happy, you can dismiss the agent without penalty or further obligation. This means you are not signing a 'locked-in' contract. Honest and decent agents will always offer you such a guarantee (if you ask for it).

2. *a price guarantee.* If the agent sells your home below the lowest quote given to you before they list your home, the agent will either agree to forfeit their commission entirely or receive whatever amount the seller chooses to pay. The beauty of this guarantee is that it forces agents to be more truthful with their initial quote.

3. *a quality guarantee.* This is a guarantee that an agent will perform certain tasks in a professional and competent manner. The agent will list the tasks they agree to undertake, together with the methods they use. This is an excellent way of making sure agents live up to their promises.

# 36 Which is better, a rookie or an experienced agent?

In many cases, rookies are better than experienced agents. Generally, rookies are more idealistic, more honest, more energetic and, most importantly, more enthusiastic. They are eager to please.

The cynicism, corruption and, worst of all, the selfishness and greed that infects many (not all) experienced agents is usually lacking in rookies. Their early idealism has not morphed into what experienced agents see as reality: the necessity of deception to achieve success. I liken it to the character Relling from one of Henrik Ibsen's plays, *The Wild Duck*, who said, 'Don't use that foreign word *ideals*; we have a good native word, *lies*'.

Many experienced agents are consummate liars. It's how they keep their careers alive and how they earn their income.

As Malone in *The Untouchables* said to Eliot Ness, who was despairing at finding an honest cop in Chicago during the bootlegging days, 'If you're afraid of getting a rotten apple don't go to the barrel; get it off the tree'.

# 37 What are agents really like?

To answer this question, here's a satire on six types of agents. Some are a mix of types.

- *Type 1: Donny Direct.* This agent doesn't care about anything but price. He'll tell you how honest he is as he hits you with a price that's like a punch in the solar plexus. If you don't like Donny's price, too bad — find another agent.
- *Type 2: Larry the Liar.* If his lips are moving, Larry is lying. From telling you how much he adores your home to the

stratospheric price he'll get for you: it's all lies. Once you list with Larry, the lies increase. They won't cease until the 'Sold' sticker appears on the sign.

- *Type 3: False Freddy.* You will likely hear Freddy before you see him. The roar of his shiny European car as he hurtles down your street is a prelude of what to expect. Everything about Freddy is phoney. Don't be drawn in by his boasts and bravado. He'll profit at your expense.
- *Type 4: Naïve Neddy.* This agent has fallen for every line trainers have taught him. He can't think for himself, so he trots out one cliché after another and hopes to sign up as many sellers as possible. He's rejected more often than he's accepted. And he hasn't figured out why.
- *Type 5: Sucker Siddy.* This agent sells in reverse. He doesn't talk *you* into anything, but anyone can talk *him* into anything. If you want too much for your home Sid seems like your man. But watch out: buyers will convince him that your home should be sold cheaply to them.
- *Type 6: The Winner.* This agent may not sell the most houses, but she will get you the most for your home. And the best part about winning agents is that they only charge you once they have succeeded. The Winners place your interests before their own.

# 38 If the agent is not on RateMyAgent, what does this mean?

It probably means the agent does not want to pay RateMyAgent. It may also be that the agent has the integrity to reject a website that contains many fake reviews and, worse, does not allow negative reviews from most unhappy sellers.

# 39 What's a common complaint sellers make about agents?

The most common complaint sellers make about agents is that the agents continually pressure them to lower their price. The agent, who initially praised and admired their home, now constantly mentions its faults. The agent gives reasons why the owners are unlikely to get the price they expected. Agents absolve themselves from any responsibility by blaming the market.

It's not the agent's fault, according to the agent. It's the market's fault and the sellers are urged to 'listen to the market'.

Another common complaint is that sellers say the agents are working for the buyers instead of them, the sellers. Most agents work for themselves. They are chasing their commission. And the fastest way to get their commission is to get a home sold as quickly as possible. At any price.

Yet another common complaint about agents from local homeowners (who are not yet selling their homes) is that they are repeatedly approached by agents looking for homes to sell. A lot of owners swear off these agents.

> *And yet, ironically, agents who chase new listings the hardest are often the hardest working agents.*

So, don't make the mistake of calling an agent who never approaches you. You could be choosing the laziest agent. Even though you may see some agents who chase you constantly as pests, these could be the best agents to chase buyers when you sell your home.

Don't ignore hard workers.

# 40 How should I treat real estate agents?

Treat agents well. Try to be courteous.

If you are rude or facetious or if you say you don't trust them (you can think it, but don't say it), they are not likely to strive to get you the highest price.

It's harder to cheat people who treat you well. If the agent genuinely likes you the first time you meet, that will bode well for your future relationship.

Try to find an agent who is interested in you as a person. Good agents are good listeners.

Despite this, do not be afraid to question agents. You are the employer. They will earn thousands of dollars if you hire them. Some may say, 'What is this — a job interview?' In which case you should reply, 'Yes, it is, and we have a lot of agents applying for the job as our agent. We want the best agent'.

At this point, bad agents will squirm. The good agents will rise to the challenge. Especially if you are courteous.

# 41 Why do agents ask how much I want for my home?

Once agents know the lowest price you will accept, they know the least amount of work they need to do. The less you want for your home, the less work the agent has to do.

The price you want is none of an agent's business. Indeed, it's no-one's business except yours and your family's or trusted advisor's. What benefit is there in revealing the lowest price you want for your home? None.

As happens at auctions, when sellers are forced to reveal their lowest price (their reserve), this becomes the agent's entire focus. The lowest you want can soon become the highest you get.

Instead of asking you what price you want for your house, the agent should be asking buyers what price the buyers will pay for your house.

And don't fall for the seemingly innocuous question that agents need to know what price you want so they know what price to aim for.

The price you want is simple. It's the best price in the marketplace. Nothing less.

# 42 What do I want an agent to do?

Here are the two things you must insist that an agent does for you.

1.  *Safety.* Your protection must be a priority. The agent must allow you to delete all (standard) nasty clauses that appear in most listing agreements.

    If the agent won't agree to this condition, don't hire them.
2.  *Price.* The agent must have the skills to ensure your home sells for the highest market price on the day it's sold.

    If the agent doesn't possess the basic skills to get you the best price, don't hire them.

# 43 Are agent-finder services or sites worthwhile?

No, definitely not. The internet is peppered with companies that claim to help home sellers to find the best or the cheapest agents. None of these companies have ethical or competency standards for agents. Their only standard is that the agent is prepared to pay these companies a share of the agent's commission.

Agent-finding companies are like those travel booking sites that ravage the profits of motels.

Most home sellers who fall into the trap of using an agent-finding site do not get a special deal. Indeed, they don't get anything special except an agent who has to pay a fee to the agent-finding company.

Many of the country's best agents refuse to be associated with agent-finding companies. If you want an agent who will treat you well, learn how to recognise such agents. For example, those who charge nothing until you sell. And those who do not hold you to a locked-in contract.

Stay away from agent-finding companies — unless they place ethical standards upon the agents they recommend and can demonstrate that you will get a better price with their help.

# 44 How can I recognise the best agents to trust?

These three words can help you recognise the best agents: *pay on success*.

The best agents neither expect nor demand *any* reward until they sell your home.

In the unlikely event that one of the best agents fails to sell your home, you will not be thousands of dollars out of pocket. You will not be sued by the agent (or one of their affiliated companies) for not paying needless marketing costs. You will not have a caveat lodged on your home. Best of all, the value of your home will be protected.

The best agents respect your finances and the value of your home.

As well as being competent, the best agents are confident. They don't need money upfront because they know you will admire their efforts, their integrity and, best of all, their results.

It's not easy to find the best agents. You may need to search long and hard. But it is better to spend three to four weeks searching for the best agent than three or four months stuck with one of the worst agents.

The agent you can trust is the one worth trusting. And not based on what they say, or their 'profile', or how many properties they've sold, or how many (often fake) reviews they've got.

You can know which agents you can trust by knowing what they do — not what they say they'll do. You aren't interested in promises. You want real results. You don't want to get ripped off.

There are seven ways to recognise trustworthy agents:

1.  They are pleasant and well-presented. You feel you can trust them.
2.  They take a genuine interest in your home and your circumstances.
3.  They never ask you for money (especially for advertising) before your home is sold. This is what is meant by 'pay on success'.
4.  They offer you a *guarantee*. You are not locked in. If you are not happy, you can leave.
5.  You are impressed by their knowledge and understanding of negotiation.

6. They are nothing like most agents. They stand out for their uniqueness.
7. They work hard. The best agents offer a seven-day service.

# 45 How can I recognise agents who are good negotiators?

Here are eight ways you can recognise agents who are good negotiators.

1. *They charge only on success.* Good negotiators have confidence in their ability. They don't demand upfront money for any reason. If a good negotiator fails to sell your home, you will not lose thousands of dollars. Good negotiators are good businesspeople. They carry the risk; they don't pass it on to their sellers.

2. *They reject public auctions.* Good negotiators don't recommend public auctions as the best way to sell. Agents who are poor negotiators are the most likely ones to recommend public auctions. Competent agents do not recommend public auctions.

3. *They accept silent auctions.* Good negotiators may suggest a silent auction. This means that, unlike a public auction, each buyer is prevented from knowing the offers of other buyers. Therefore, each buyer is compelled to offer their highest price. This ensures that homes sell for thousands of dollars more.

4. *They are hard workers.* Good negotiators work hard. It takes a lot more time, energy and skill to negotiate privately with multiple buyers. Lazy agents round up all buyers at a public auction and spend 20 to 30 minutes yelling at them. This is not the way to get the best price. Sitting comfortably in

somebody's home and discussing the merits of various homes is the best way to get the best price. Lazy agents reject such methods with all sorts of excuses. But hard-working agents will do whatever it takes to obtain the last dollar on behalf of their sellers.

5. *They are not cheap*. Agents who get the best prices are great negotiators. They have invested hundreds, perhaps thousands, of hours (and dollars) learning negotiation. They get the best price and expect the best commission. To be sure, good negotiators are ethical. If they cannot get a better price than a typical agent, they will not charge more than a typical agent.

6. *They don't accept everyone*. Most agents will accept any sellers under any conditions and then condition them down in price later. Good negotiators will not do this. In return for their fairness, they expect the same from clients. Good negotiation involves plenty of work. So, it's important to the good agents that their clients be onside. Good negotiators and good sellers are a winning combination.

7. *They have impressive knowledge*. Ask agents to give you examples of how they negotiate. If you're not impressed, they're not good negotiators. The best negotiators are impressive with their knowledge. They know how to get the best prices.

8. *They know your home*. Good negotiators know that knowledge is power. The more they know about your home the more likely they are to get you a better price. Some agents barely glance at the features of a home. The best agents, the ones skilled at negotiation, take time to learn the features of your home.

# 46 What should I ask agents who want to list my home?

Here are 20 questions (each with a comment) to ask agents when you interview them.

1. *Why do you feel you are the best agent to sell my home?* Be careful of agents who boast about their success. Top agents rarely get top prices. Their major skill is conditioning sellers down in price. They rarely negotiate in your best interests.

    You need an agent who cares about clients.

2. *How much commission do you charge and are you prepared to discount it?* This is almost a trick question. The agent who offers a cheap commission and is quick to discount it even further is probably not the best agent. If agents give their own money away, they are not likely to protect your money.

3. *Do you have buyers who you believe would be interested in my home right now?* Agents will often gush about all the buyers on their books. They may claim to have 'leftover buyers' from previously sold homes. You can have access to these buyers if you sign up with them. Make sure you hold them to this promise. Therefore, make sure that you sign up for no more than two weeks. You don't want a situation where the agent promises they have lots of buyers, but after you sign up, those buyers disappear. You are then asked to pay thousands of dollars in advertising to find buyers. Many sellers are tricked in this manner.

4. *What do you believe is a realistic price for which I can sell my property?* Make it clear that you understand that agents have a motive to overquote the likely selling price of your home. Tell them that you are realistic, and you don't expect anything other than the best they can do. Be careful that you do not reward an agent for lying to you.

5. *If you quote me a high price and then, after I sign up, you push me to sell at a lower price, will you charge a lower commission percentage, given that your commission is high, regardless of the final selling price?* This question can make agents squirm. You'll likely enjoy their response.

6. *Do you offer any form of guarantee?* A guarantee is a basic consumer right. But you don't get a guarantee from most agents. This is a shameful aspect of the real estate industry. The best agents offer guarantees; if they don't, they will happily agree to one designed by you.

7. *If one of my relatives wants to buy my home, do I still have to pay you commission?* If you put this question directly to agents, it's hard for them to look you in the eye and tell you they still want maximum pay for zero work.

8. *Are you okay with a Sole Agency Agreement (which gives the seller the flexibility to sell the property privately if they find a buyer independently) instead of an Exclusive Agency Agreement? If not, why not?* The game is up when you ask a question like this. The agent will realise they're dealing with somebody who understands real estate. Any agent who refuses a Sole Agency Agreement and insists on an Exclusive Agency Agreement should be rejected.

9.  *Why do you need to know the lowest price I will accept?* If an agent insists on knowing your lowest price or the price you want (same thing), you can reply, 'I want the best price in today's market'.

10. *Do you consider yourself a good negotiator?* Every agent will say 'yes' to this question. But taking offers back and forth between sellers and buyers is not negotiation. That's simply being a messenger.

    And worse, pushing sellers down in price is not negotiation. It's bullying.

    You need to know how an agent can get buyers up in price, not push sellers down in price.

    Ask them.

11. *Would you mind telling me what you know about negotiation?* Beware of clichés. When agents discuss negotiation skills, the three words you need to hear in your mind are these: 'I am impressed'.

    If you are not impressed, you haven't found the right agent yet.

12. *Do you think selling by auction is the best way to sell?* The answer you are hoping to hear is, 'No, definitely not. Never'.

    If an agent says that auction is the best way to sell — or even says that on some occasions auction is the best way to sell — ask them if they have read the book *88 Reasons Why You Must Never Sell Your Home at Auction*. They may ask if that is one of my books. If you say yes, they may tell you they haven't read it, but they'll criticise it, in which case you need to then ask, 'How can you criticise something you haven't read?'

13. *What method of sale do you recommend?* Any method that involves qualifying buyers (see question 162) and discovering the highest price they're willing to pay (not just for your property but any property) is the best method.

14. *What are your operating hours?* Reject agents that are only open Monday to Friday and closed on weekends. Ideally, you want an agent who is open seven days. That's because buyers are mostly available after hours and on weekends.

15. *If I list with your agency how many agents will I have working on my home?* Sellers who list with a large agency often think they'll get dozens of agents working on their home. This is a huge trap. With most big-name companies you are restricted to one salesperson — the one with whom you listed. The other agents are forbidden from going near your home. The agency does what's best for individual agents, not individual sellers.

16. *If you ask me to pay advertising money and you get leads from my ads that give you sales, do I get some of the commission from those sales, or do you keep it all for yourself?* If you are an assertive and knowledgeable seller who enjoys seeing arrogant agents squirm, you will love this question. It exposes the unfairness of the VPA (vendor paid advertising) system (see question 134).

    It's near heartbreaking to hear fair and decent home sellers accept the premise that 'because it's their home they should pay the advertising costs'. Most sellers have no idea how agents profit by extracting advertising dollars from sellers.

17. *Are you okay to leave your paperwork with me and give me a few days to read it carefully?* You need to read most agents' listing contracts with a magnifying glass. Take your time. You will likely discover clauses and fine-print conditions that will make you feel betrayed even before you start to sell your home.

    If the agent will not leave their paperwork with you, reject the agent.

18. *Are you okay if I add conditions to your Listing Agreement and delete any I feel are unfair?* Any agent who does not reply with an enthusiastic 'yes' to this question is not an agent you can trust. Do not accept excuses such as 'company policy'. All contracts can be amended.

    Make sure the listing contracts are amended to suit you.

19. *If I am not happy with you, can I terminate your services without penalties or obligations?* With most agents, definitely not. Once you sign up, you are locked in no matter what the agent does or how the agent treats you.

    An exit clause guarantee is another basic consumer right. It's not just common sense — it's common decency. If you don't like a person, you shouldn't be forced to be in a relationship with them.

20. *Are you all right with me using Jenman Support to help?* If an agent says no, be concerned. If they say they cannot afford to pay the support fee because it reduces their commission (they're not allowed to increase their commission to cover the Jenman Support fee), then you have our permission to ask, 'But what if Jenman Support agrees to donate their fee from you to charity. Will that be okay?' You might also ask them if they too would donate their fee to a worthy charity.

# 47 What happens if an agent won't agree to my listing terms?

Don't consider agents who won't agree to your terms.

You are the employer. You hire the agent under your terms. The agent is your employee. And employees don't dictate unreasonable terms to their employers, as happens with most real estate agents in Australia.

Stand up for yourself.

# 48 When an agent is pitching to list my home, how long do I give them?

Someone once said that the reason you should take an immediate dislike to real estate agents is because it saves time. It's often true. However, unless you are totally repulsed when you first meet an agent, it's always good to hear them out. Give them as much time as you need. You should spend at least one and a half hours with each agent.

Ask as many questions as you like. Treat this as an interview. Just as if you are an employer looking for a good employee. That is *exactly* what is happening.

Never forget, however, that the agent's aim is to sign you up. The best way to 'list' you is by telling you what you want to hear — especially the sale price of your home.

Be careful.

# 49 Should I sell through my rental agent or a different agent?

When selling any property, always choose the agent who is likely to achieve the best result.

While your loyalty to your rental agent might be admirable, such loyalty could be expensive. Just because an agent is a good rental agent, it does not mean they are a good selling agent. It's rare to find an agent who's good at both renting and selling properties.

Put loyalty to your rental agent aside and place your loyalty where it belongs: with you and your family.

The answer is simple: hire the agent most likely to get the best result.

# 50 Is it true that out-of-area agents often get better prices?

A common mistake made by home sellers is insisting on using a local agent.

If more sellers realised that foreign (out-of-area) agents can do a better job than local agents, more sellers would get more money for their homes. Generally, the worst thing you can do is hire a local agent. These agents are often so price prejudiced they can't think outside the proverbial box. They believe certain homes can't be sold in their area for more than certain prices. And these prices often have nothing to do with reality and everything to do with whatever is inside the closed minds of such local agents.

Time after time it happens: an agent from outside an area sells a home in a different area for a price far above what local agents predicted.

This law is not rock solid, however. Some local agents are excellent. They fight like tigers to get the best price for sellers in their area. And they never charge until homes have been successfully sold.

But if you are having trouble with local agents, try a foreign agent. It could be the best way to get the best price.

# 51 Should I use a network agent or an independent agent?

Most real estate agencies are independently owned and operated — including those with a major franchise.

Given a choice between an independent or a big-brand agent, the better choice is usually the independent one. Big-brand agencies are renowned for low ethical standards. Their entire focus is on building their brand, not on building customer relations.

Remember, however, you are usually dealing with one person regardless of whether the agency is a small business or part of a chain. If that person agrees to your terms and also has the skills to get you the best price, this is the agent you should consider.

# 52 Should I use the top-selling agent in the area?

Choosing a top-selling agent does not mean you get the best price.

Real estate is ruthlessly competitive. Those who rise to the top are often the most ruthless.

Sure, a few agents are honest and competent.

You need to know the difference between agents who genuinely care about you and those who care more about GCI (gross commission income). GCI is explained in detail in question 73.

# 53 Should I use a discount agent?

Preferably not. Here's why…

If the main way you choose an agent is on their commission rate, you are making a common mistake.

A sure sign of an agent being a poor negotiator is that they can't negotiate for themselves. A cheap agent often means cheap prices.

You need an agent who gets you the highest price, not one who charges the lowest commission. Of course, you may think you can get an agent to sell your house for a high price and charge you a low commission. It seldom happens.

Consider this: What's more important to you? The amount that goes in your pocket or the amount that goes in the agent's pocket?

Surely you should choose the agent who puts the most money in your pocket and then — once you see how they perform — you can negotiate how much the agent deserves in their pocket. Always focus on the upside for you.

# 54 Is it worth using a vendors' advocate?

A vendors' advocate purportedly helps vendors (sellers) choose a good agent. The advocate is supposed to advise sellers on the best method of sale and how to find the best buyer.

During the selling process, the advocate should ensure that the agent always acts in the best interests of the seller. The advocate should also assist the seller when it comes to the all-important task of negotiating the best price.

Unfortunately, the main motive of many advocates is the same as many agents: money. Worse, some advocates—especially those 'find-the-best-agent' websites—select agents who offer the best deal to the advocate.

If, however, you can find a vendors' advocate who is competent and honest, it may be worth engaging one.

Scott Kim—an agent in the Monash area of suburban Melbourne—gets far higher prices for his home sellers than other agents get for similar homes (especially those agents who push public auctions). Scott does not think highly of vendors' advocates. These are his comments:

> Vendors' advocates are mostly of no benefit to sellers because they focus on sending sellers to [the] agents who pay them the most money. This is just another example of the many blatant conflicts of interest in real estate where these advocates advise sellers to choose a method or path that leads to more money for the advocates and usually a lower price for the home sellers.

For example, many vendors' advocates recommend public auction to their sellers knowing that homes are often massively undersold at auctions.

So, hiring an advocate on the basis that you'll get good advice is nonsensical if they give you bad advice. Sure, they may argue that they charge the seller nothing (because the agent pays their fee). But they can cost you plenty if your home is undersold.

# 55 How can I find an honest and competent vendors' advocate?

If you do decide to use a vendors' advocate, the best way to choose a competent one is to test their knowledge. One way to test their knowledge is by asking questions (of yourself and of them).

## Questions to ask yourself

- *How did I find this vendors' advocate?* The best way to find a trustworthy advocate is via a recommendation from someone you trust.
- *Do I like this advocate as a person?* Be careful of anyone who tells you what you want to hear. Look at how they act, how they dress, how they speak. Even the car they drive. This might sound nugatory, but would you want them in your family? Even temporarily. After all, they may have a powerful influence on your family's finances.
- *Am I impressed by this person's knowledge?* As well as being impressed by what they tell you, are they telling you something positive and beneficial that you did not know? Beware of real estate clichés.

## Questions to ask an advocate

- *Why should I choose your services?* Ask them to be specific about how they can help you. In particular, you are concerned with three aspects. First, protecting you from stress; second, protecting you from being overcharged; and finally, ensuring you get the best sale price.

- *What criteria do you use when selecting an agent?* Nothing is more important than finding an agent who will negotiate the highest price without charging you needless expenses (like upfront advertising).

- *What method of sale is best?* Listen carefully to the answer. Many advocates try to be all things to all people. They lack either the courage or the knowledge to criticise ineffective methods.

- *What do you know about Jenman Support?* Almost all agents have never read a book on the most important subject they need to assist sellers: the art of negotiation. Their ignorance is on display to anyone who researches real estate selling methods.

  Over decades in the real estate industry, I have attended many customer care courses. I have read hundreds of books. I have listened to the seminars of dozens of real estate and business gurus from all over the world. I have studied ethics, philosophy and literature and applied many principles in my life. My primary aim has always been to place the interests of clients ahead of my own interests. And to always strive to be kind, especially to the less fortunate.

  If an agent or advocate does not study their profession, they are unlikely to be good at providing excellent service to their clients.

  There have been more than two million copies of my books published. Most are read by consumers, who appreciate what they discover. Many agents criticise me without reading a single one of my books.

  If an advocate is not well read on how to help real estate consumers, they are unlikely to be a worthwhile advocate.

- *Do you place conditions on the agent to protect my interests?* A competent advocate will insist that an agent delete all nasty clauses in the Listing Agreement. The advocate will also insist that the agent inserts clauses that protect the seller. For example, the advocate will insist that the owner maintains the right to sell privately. The advocate will also make sure that the owners are not locked into a selling agreement if the agent turns out to be unsuitable.

In summary, the advocate makes sure the seller — not the agent — has control.

# 56 Should I hire an agent who is open seven days?

Most definitely, yes. That's if you can find an agent smart enough and hard-working enough to be available when buyers are most available, namely weekends and after hours.

Laziness is endemic in the real estate world. It is largely caused by the extraordinarily high commissions agents earn. Many agents get paid a lot for doing very little. So why work more than necessary? If they can earn upwards of $250 000 a year working from nine to five on five days a week, that's all many do.

Most buyers work from Monday to Friday and from 9 am to 5 pm. The best time for these buyers to inspect homes for sale is after working hours — say between 5 pm and 7 pm on weekdays. On Saturdays and Sundays, most buyers are free to view homes. Incredibly, most agents close when most buyers are available.

You should reject all agents who close at 5 pm during the week and who are closed all weekend. These are not just lazy agents; they are also stupid. No intelligent business owner would shut out their customers when those customers are most available.

# 57 Must I sign up with an agent for three or four months?

No. You are not compelled to sign up with an agent for any set time.

Agents want to sign you up for as long as possible. But unless you have complete trust in the agent, you should never sign up for more than 30 days. If the agent yelps at this condition, tell them that, provided their work is satisfactory, you will extend the Listing Agreement for another 30 days. Keep re-extending every 30 days until your home is sold. This will prevent you being trapped for months with an agent you don't like. It will also motivate the agent to treat you well.

# 58 If other agents offer to match their competitors, should I consider using them?

When pushed, some agents agree to break from their usual dodgy methods. Especially if they look like losing business to an agent who specialises in a better method.

If an agent usually uses methods that are not the best for sellers but agrees to make an exception in your case and treat you well, be wary. As the saying goes, leopards don't change their spots.

The agents you should never use, however, are those who claim to use ethical methods but clearly don't.

# 59 If I sign up with an experienced agent, will I be delegated to a junior?

The greatest 'sell' in the real estate world is 'selling sellers to list their homes'. This task often goes to the slickest agent.

Once the seller signs up, the slick agent is rarely seen again. The seller is handed to an inexperienced agent.

The way to avoid this trap is to ensure that the salesperson who signs you up is the salesperson who will look after you for the duration of the sale process. Ask the direct question, 'Will you be looking after me or will I be delegated to less senior agents?'

Be careful. Most top agents drop sellers once they list.

# 60 Can I list with more than one agent?

Yes, you can list with many agents. You can 'open list' with as many agents as will accept your listing. Most agents refuse such listings, however.

Open listings are more common in the bush than in cities.

Many years ago, when homeowners wanted to sell, their first stop was at a hardware store, not at an agent. The owners would get a dozen keys cut for their home. They would give keys to several agents and say, 'Whoever sells my home first — and for the best price — gets the commission'.

Of course, many agents don't like hard work at the best of times. These days very few will work on an open listing because, unlike an exclusive listing, there is no guarantee they will get paid.

Agents like guarantees — that is, getting them, not giving them.

# 61 What can happen after I sign an agent's Listing Agreement?

Lots can happen. And although everything will hopefully go smoothly for you, it's almost impossible to exaggerate the dangers sellers face when dealing with many real estate agents — often those who appear the nicest.

So bear with me while I divulge some of what can happen if you don't delete the unconscionable clauses in the agent's Listing Agreement.

- You could end up with your home unsold and be thousands of dollars out of pocket for needless marketing costs. If you become annoyed and refuse to pay the agent or one of the agent's related companies, they may place a caveat on your home. This means you cannot sell your home without paying thousands of dollars that you have been unfairly charged.

- If one of your family members or a friend buys your home, you still have to pay the agent.

- You may have to tolerate the agent's almost schizophrenic change in personality after you sign up. Smiles are replaced by frowns. Positives are replaced by negatives. Worst of all, the estimated sale price tumbles. If you originally signed up because you were excited by the agent's selling price estimate, but you are now being asked to accept a much lower price, there is little you can do. If you withdraw from the sale, you may receive a bill for thousands of dollars in advertising.

- Your home is probably uninsured when being inspected. (Check your insurance policy.) So if the agent has an accident on your property — or does anything wrong — even if it is their fault, you are liable for all losses and damages.

- If you fail to give the agent a written termination notice in accordance with the complicated conditions in the Listing Agreement and you hire another agent who sells your property, you may be liable for two commissions.
- Most agents act as introduction agents. If somebody inspects your property and doesn't buy it because the agent lacks the sales skill, and then, a few months later, the same person buys your home thanks to a skilled agent, the first agent can also claim a commission.
- Many agents get huge kickbacks (or bonus benefits) on money they urge you to spend. Some agents get a bigger percentage for selling advertising to sellers than for selling homes to buyers.
- If, for any reason, you decide not to sell, the agent can still charge you commission. This can apply if the agent has found a buyer at the price you expected — regardless of whether you allow the buyer to proceed. The agents can say they are paid to 'find a buyer' and that's exactly what they did.
- If you decide you don't like the agent, too bad. You're stuck with them. Once you sign up with an agent for a period of time, you can't go anywhere else without paying the agent you don't like.

> *Do not sign up with any agent until you delete all their nasty clauses!*

# 62 If negotiation skills are so important, why do so few agents learn these skills?

For decades, agents have had it easy because of near permanent property booms in many areas. They can overquote the likely price to win a listing, and in the weeks or months it takes to sell that listing, the boom in prices turns their lies into truths. Some then describe themselves as legends.

The main skill sought by agents is to convince sellers to list. It is easier to overinflate the selling price or misrepresent how many buyers they have on their books than to spend months (even years) learning to be a skilled negotiator.

It is negligent of agents not to learn a skill that could win them more business and make them more sales. It would also make them more respected. But that's the way it is. Thanks to perennial property booms, commissions have boomed. Many agents now earn huge incomes for low performance levels. Indeed, many of today's so-called 'top performers' would have been dismissed for poor performance pre-2000.

If you are interested in knowing more about real estate negotiation, you can download the 28-page booklet *The 42 Rules of Modern Real Estate Negotiation* at jenman.com.au.

# 63 How can I design a smart and effective plan to sell my home?

If you can design an effective plan for the sale of your home, you will get a much better price and pay far less in costs.

The first point to consider is *What is an effective plan?*

It's the best way to find the best buyers at the least cost. A good plan protects the value of your home.

The more advertising that's done, the more you damage the value of your home. If it doesn't sell, buyers wonder what's wrong. Then come the low offers.

But here's the point: advertising a home should be the *last* part of any plan — not the first part, as it is for so many incompetent agents.

Most agents get hundreds of enquiries from prospective buyers. Some get thousands of enquiries every month. Yet, agents rarely respond to buyer enquiries. Very few agents follow up buyers by telephone. And almost no agents call prospective buyers when a likely suitable listing comes up for sale.

Even though agents have buyers on their books, they prefer to spend the sellers' money advertising to attract buyers already known to the agents. This gives the agents two advantages. They promote themselves at the sellers' expense. Plus, they use the advertising as a conditioning weapon: 'Your home has been advertised and it hasn't sold. Therefore, the market says you need to reduce your price'.

Wrong in so many respects.

The reason the home hasn't sold is twofold: first, the agent is too lazy to call buyers; and second, the excessive advertising causes buyers to wonder what's wrong with the home.

## How to avoid advertising your home

Years ago, before the explosion in real estate advertising and before sellers were convinced to pay advertising costs, agents had to be creative. They had to find a way to find buyers without wasting their own dollars in advertising.

The first thing that agents used to do (and should still do) when they listed a home was to ask themselves, 'Who might buy this home?' Often the agents had several buyers in mind. They would return to their offices and call their top-of-mind buyers. If that didn't bring forth a suitable buyer, the agent would call other buyers, especially those who had missed out on similar properties.

For so many sales, advertising wasn't needed.

So, here is a sound and sensible plan for selling a home: *contact buyers on the books*.

Insist that the agent contacts all buyers who have shown interest in the sort of home you are offering for sale. And 'contact' does not mean sending mass emails to buyers. That's the lazy way. The best way is to have voice contact with dozens of likely buyers. Even hundreds. As many as it takes to arrange some inspections for qualified buyers. Remember, buyers often pay more for a home that has not been advertised. They are getting in ahead of other buyers. They are buying something special.

## Check your local area

The best buyers, especially for family homes, are usually locals. The closer to the home for sale, the more the chance of finding the best buyer. Locals are the most underrated source of buyers.

If you (or your agent) approach owners in the street where a home has just been listed, there's an excellent chance of finding an instant buyer. And one prepared to pay above market value.

So many times, home sellers spend thousands of dollars in marketing costs only to find that the buyer for their home was someone in their street. So, before you spend any money advertising, check the street.

And be sure you always have a For Sale sign at the front of your home. It's the cheapest and best form of promoting your home. Like a 24-hour salesperson on your lawn.

## Ask yourself why you bought

Why did you buy this home that you now want to sell? Find someone with the same motivation and interest as you. For example, if you're a schoolteacher and the home is near your school, that's a special advantage for you. If you're a doctor and the home is near a hospital, another advantage. There are many reasons why people choose homes in certain areas — anything from close to the airport to the peace of rolling hills. Find a buyer that fits your profile, and you'll likely find the right buyer. Someone just like you. Homes can sell with just a notice on a company or community noticeboard.

## Target prime prospects

Most real estate advertising is needlessly widespread. You are forced to pay thousands of dollars to reach millions of lookers. You don't want lookers — you want buyers. Indeed, you only want one buyer.

So, think of the professional people who may be interested in your home: people who value privacy and shun homes that hundreds of lookers have traipsed through. Think of where buyers go, where they hang out. And write to them.

Write to local lawyers telling them of a wonderful home for sale. Do the same with mortgage brokers who are arranging finance for buyers. Think smart. Use a laser approach to marketing. It's cheaper and more effective.

## If you must advertise

In the extremely unlikely event that you do not find the right buyer using these methods, perhaps you may consider a small advertisement. Remember, large advertisements are a waste of money.

Serious buyers are resourceful. They visit multiple websites; they type in their preferences, and they find your home. The flashier your advertising, the more it will cost you and the more it will damage the value of your home if you don't sell quickly. An inexpensive ad on social media, or a local community site for sellers and buyers, can be far more effective than paying thousands of dollars.

So, don't lose your nerve. Find an agent prepared to chase buyers. Avoid lazy agents who use your money to promote themselves and attract buyers already known to them.

If you follow these steps, you'll likely get a much higher price with much lower costs.

# 64 Do agents have a plan to sell my home?

Most agents will claim they have a plan to sell your home. Most of their plans are typical and predictable.

There's a true saying about plans: 'Pathetic planning creates pathetic results'. Most agents' plans are pathetic. That's why they achieve pathetic results.

Here's how they work.

Most agents' plans centre upon advertising. You will be given a list of websites on which to place ads, all of which charge varying sums of money (payable by you). You'll also be given a series of suggested extras (at more cost to you) such as floor plans, photography, drones and anything else agents can possibly think of to justify charging you more money.

This will be their plan.

What's described above is not a plan. It's a list of needless costs designed to promote the agent at your expense. If your home doesn't sell, the agent gets the benefit of all the free advertising (paid for by you), and you are several thousand dollars out of pocket.

These so-called plans — often called 'marketing plans' — could be more aptly named 'scam steps'.

Once the advertising has been booked, the agent arranges a series of open inspections at your home. Most agents will have your home 'open to inspect' for about half an hour per week. Yes, that's right, out of 10 080 minutes in a week, you get 30 minutes. Some agents are now down to 15 minutes.

Sellers who protest that 30 minutes is not enough time will receive one of the agent's standard pre-planned responses, such as, 'If the buyers are really interested, they'll turn up at the open-house time'. But if the open-for-inspection time does not suit the buyers, they won't show up.

Laziness and stupidity are rife in the real estate world and there is no better example of laziness and stupidity than what many agents describe as 'a plan to sell your home'.

# 65 Should I let my agent enlist the help of other agents?

Most buyers are known to all the active agents in your area. So, if your agent is the best negotiator in your area, you should not allow conjunctions with other agents. A 'conjunction' is when two agents share the commission. Often, sellers list with one agent and then a second agent produces a buyer. But the agent who's the better negotiator should always be the one who deals with the buyers.

You want to be sure that the buyer for your home negotiates with the most competent negotiator.

If, however, you suspect that your agent is less skilled than you first believed, it may be wise to suggest that your agent enlists the help of other agents.

This point is especially valid when other agents contact you claiming to have a buyer for your property and intimate that your agent is inefficient. In most cases, agents who approach you in this manner are not to be trusted. It's unlikely that they really do have a buyer who's not known to your agent, and certainly not at a better price.

However, to test the sincerity of such agents, you may insist that your agent offers them a conjunction.

If a second agent finds the right buyer for your property, both agents will share the commission — usually on a 50/50 basis. Be careful. Do not sign anything with a second agent, or you may be liable to pay double commission. If in doubt, get legal advice.

# 66 What happens if I accidentally sign up with the wrong agent?

If you sign up with most agents — and you aren't offered (or haven't insisted upon) a protection guarantee — you have four options.

First, lump it. Unfortunately, this is what most sellers do when their agent is not living up to their expectations. They tolerate it.

Second, you can approach the agent and ask to be released from the Listing Agreement. Most agents will be reticent. Others will insist you pay thousands of dollars for so-called marketing expenses before they will even consider releasing you.

Third, you can complain. But, to whom? The real estate institutes will ignore you or make excuses for the agents. The media will also likely ignore you. And regulatory authorities are often so overworked and understaffed they won't have time to investigate your complaint. You really will feel alone.

Finally, if you are determined to complain and you're prepared to incur some cost, you can consult a lawyer. Sometimes a short and stern letter from a lawyer will inspire an agent to release you. Such early action should cost you less than $1000. It's certainly a better option than staying with an agent who will undersell your home by tens of thousands of dollars.

# 67 Is 'introducing' a buyer the same as 'selling' my home?

Great question.

You are dealing with a real estate agency, not an introduction agency. This may seem obvious. But read the fine print in most Listing Agreements and you'll see a seemingly harmless word: 'introduce'. Look out.

Here's what can happen.

An incompetent agent shows a home to some buyers (or stands at a front door and waves them in). The buyers seem keen. But the agent only has time to grab their details before rushing to another open house. In the following days, the buyers make several attempts to contact the agent without success. Eventually, they give up.

Fast forward six weeks. The sellers have changed agents. Their new agent is efficient. The same buyers contact this agent and ask for an inspection. Later, they decide to buy the home.

Another six weeks go by. The sellers move out, and the buyers move in.

The first agent sees that the home has been sold to 'their' buyers (the ones he 'introduced' months ago; the ones he ignored). The first agent now demands full commission.

The sellers must now pay two commissions to two agents. One to the efficient agent who sold their home and one to the inefficient agent who did not sell their home. All because of a sneaky (but dangerous) word: 'introduce'.

You need to hire a sales agent, not an introduction agent. Ensure the Listing Agreement confirms this vital point.

# 68 Why do agents 'knock' other agents?

Agents often denigrate their competitors. It's the sleazy nature of real estate. If, however, you find that almost all the agents seem to be critical of one agent — even to the point of warning you about that agent — perhaps you should consider that agent.

It's generally true that the more popular agents are with clients, the more disliked they will be by other agents. The most hated agent (by other agents) is often the best agent.

Make sure you understand the difference between denigrating a person and denigrating a system or method. Many real estate methods warrant severe criticism.

## Key takeaways from part 3

▶ It is not essential to use an agent when selling your home. If you can't find a great agent, consider selling without one. It's not hard and you will almost certainly get a better price with fewer costs.

▶ 'Typical' agents are common. They lock you in, undersell your home and overcharge.

▶ Agents who are skilled negotiators get much better prices for their sellers.

▶ Consider mystery-shopping agents before choosing one.

(continued)

- The best agents offer a guarantee. If you are not happy, you can dismiss the agent with no financial cost or obligation.
- Rookie agents are often a better option than experienced agents.
- Foreign (out-of-area) agents often get better prices.
- Be warned: the website RateMyAgent is funded by agents. Many unhappy sellers find it impossible to leave negative reviews on this site.
- Treat agents with courtesy regardless of how you feel about them.
- The worst agents will push you to reveal the lowest price (or any price) you are hoping for. Don't tell them what that is.
- Agent-finder sites are rarely in your best interests.
- There are seven ways to pick the best agents, all of whom are 'pay on success'.
- Focus on the 20 questions to ask agents.
- You choose how long you wish to sign up for. If you're unsure, limit the time to 30 days.
- Understand how to prepare a plan for the sale of your home.
- Always read the fine print around what happens when an agent 'introduces' a buyer. Be careful you aren't forced to pay two lots of commission!
- If most agents seem to denigrate the same agent, make sure you meet that agent.

# PART 4

# UNDERSTANDING COMMISSION AND COSTS

This part will explain real estate commissions in a unique and pragmatic manner. You will see how smart sellers inspire agents to work hard to sell homes for the best price.

But first, a warning.

One of the biggest mistakes made by home sellers is choosing an agent who offers the cheapest commission.

Cheap agents are often the most expensive because they sell your home for a cheap price. If an agent can't negotiate a good fee for themselves, they are not likely to negotiate a good price for your home. If they give their own money away, what do you think will happen if you put them in charge of your money?

By the time you have read and understood the questions and answers in this part of the book, you will be able to choose the agent who offers value for the commission you choose to pay.

# Questions in this part

69. What is the most important word to consider regarding commission?
70. What are the three costs of selling?
71. How much commission do agents charge?
72. What is the average commission percentage?
73. What is GCI?
74. How many hours of work are involved in the sale of a home?
75. All agents are alike, so why not use one who quotes a high selling price and a low commission?
76. If the agent sells my home for less than they quote, do I pay less commission?
77. The agent sold my home quickly. Shouldn't I get a commission discount?
78. How do I get an agent to give me a commission discount?
79. When should I negotiate the commission?
80. Must I pay for advertising *plus* commission?
81. Do agents get a higher commission for a higher sale price?
82. Could I be forced to pay double commission?
83. Is it a mistake to shop around looking for the cheapest commission rate?
84. Can a higher commission really get me a higher sale price?
85. What is a bonus fee — and how does it work?
86. Are there any catches with bonus fees?
87. Are there other costs on top of the commission?
88. What are the different fees some agents try to charge?
89. What is the fairest commission rate — for agents and owners?

# 69 What is the most important word to consider regarding commission?

*Justify.*

Here is how you use the word 'justify'.

Can the agent justify their rate of commission? If an agent charges 1 per cent (or even 2 per cent) more than other agents, and yet this agent consistently sells homes for 10 to 15 per cent more than other agents, the justification is proven.

It makes great sense to use an agent with a higher commission if the agent does indeed get higher prices for homes.

# 70 What are the three costs of selling?

There are three costs associated with the sale of most homes:

- The first is the commission cost.
- The second cost is the big one. It's the amount by which a home is undersold, usually due to an agent's lack of negotiation skills.

  Most properties are undersold, generally by at least 10 per cent of the selling price. Therefore, a home that sells for $1 million could most likely have sold for $1.1 million. And while the owners focus on the $20 000 commission (being 2 per cent of $1 million), most never realise they have undersold by $100 000.
- The third cost of selling a home is the cost of needless marketing expenses. You should never agree to pay such expenses unless your home is sold and you're satisfied that the

marketing expenses are justified. And never agree to pay for marketing costs if your home is not sold.

Only naïve home sellers get stung for thousands of dollars in marketing costs.

# 71 How much commission do agents charge?

Since the late 1990s, real estate commission rates have been deregulated in all areas of Australia. This has meant that commissions have increased, not decreased as the regulatory authorities were led to believe. With the enormity of commissions these days — where some agents pocket hundreds of thousands of dollars for selling one home — it's likely that commission rates may soon become regulated again.

Until then, many agents will continue to charge as much as they can get away with. It's sad but true: elderly widows often pay more commission than hard-nosed businesspeople.

In Australia, the average commission is around 2 per cent of the sale price. In some areas, agents charge as much as 3 or 4 per cent. On small blocks or cheap properties, commission may be as high as 5 per cent.

There are a few areas where the commission seems extraordinarily high and none of the agents give a discount. This can mean that agents have colluded to keep commission rates higher. This is known as a 'cartel'. If you suspect this is happening in your area, you can complain to the ACCC.

In upmarket areas — where sale prices start at $5 million and can exceed $50 million — it's common to see commission rates as low as half a per cent. But here's an astounding fact: in high-end suburbs, where the most important factor to agents is their profile, some agents charge zero commission for the prestige of selling a well-known home. The higher the agents' egos, the lower their commission.

# 72 What is the average commission percentage?

As we saw in question 71, the average commission in Australia is 2 per cent. With the average home in Australia now worth around $1 million, that's $20 000 per home.

New Zealand agents earn as much as 4 per cent commission. Plus, they are now emulating many of the dodgy practices of Australia's agents such as auctions and VPA (vendor paid advertising), which is explained in question 134.

In France, the average commission is 5 per cent. But in France, more than 50 per cent of homes are sold without an agent.

In England, the average commission is 1.2 per cent.

In the United States, agents' commission is around 6 per cent, but buyers often pay half, which effectively means sellers pay 3 per cent.

In China, home of legendary negotiators, the average commission is 1 per cent.

In essence, you can pay whatever commission rate you decide to pay. It's always best to negotiate the commission, however, *after* the agent finds a buyer for your home. To do this, you can add the words 'Negotiable until the point of unconditional sale'. These words should be written beside the agent's suggested commission rate on the Listing Agreement. Please remember that any conditions in a Listing Agreement can be changed prior to unconditional sale (provided both you and the agent agree).

Don't remove their incentive (and inspiration) prior to the sale. See what sort of a job they do. And then decide what you feel they are worth.

# 73 What is GCI?

In the 21st century, GCI has become the common lexicon of agents. It stands for 'gross commission income'.

Real estate groups provide agents with a phone app to view how thousands of their fellow agents rank... in GCI, of course.

The entire industry is focused on GCI. Agents are judged on GCI. Awards are based on GCI.

When agents meet each other, they don't ask, 'How are you?' They ask, 'What's your GCI?'

GCI is the beginning, the middle and the end of almost everything in the modern real estate world. There are rarely awards for client service and there is no known recognition for ethical and decent agents. Indeed, when ethics courses are offered to agents, they are usually cancelled due to lack of interest.

## The name of the game

Many agents are like the movie character played by Matthew McConaughey in *The Wolf of Wall Street* when he says, 'F__ the clients. Your only responsibility is to put meat on the table'. He then adds, 'Name of the game: move the money from your client's pocket into your pocket'.

Indeed, when the real so-called 'Wolf of Wall Street', Jordan Belfort, spoke at a real estate conference in Australia, thousands of agents flocked to hear him speak. They laughed, they cheered, they clapped—and then they mobbed him as if he was a rock star and not a criminal who spent 22 months in prison for fraud.

# 74 How many hours of work are involved in the sale of a home?

Usually less than 10 hours. Sometimes as little as four hours—if you exclude the time spent at the listing presentation.

Even less for an auction sale. Consider four open for inspections at 30 minutes each and then 60 minutes on auction day. That's three hours. And often the open for inspections are delegated to a junior—especially if you've listed your home with a so-called top agent.

With the average commission now $20000 or more—and often more than $100000 in upmarket areas—agents can earn a hefty income. For doing very little. Or so it seems.

Work it out. That's $2000 an hour for 10 hours of work. For an average property.

Or an auction on an upmarket home could work out at around $25000 an hour.

Little wonder the industry is crawling with agents. But, before you get too judgemental, remember that what you are paying for is the agent's *effectiveness*. You need to consider their *ability* to get you the *highest market price*.

Can you justify paying an agent $100000 commission for four hours' work? Well, if the agent negotiated $1 million more than you expected (or accepted), maybe.

But if you have a property where the commission is $20000 and the agent sells it at or below the standard market price, they likely haven't done anything you couldn't do yourself.

Think before you sign.

# 75 All agents are alike, so why not use one who quotes a high selling price and a low commission?

All agents are not alike.

The difference between the best agents and the worst agents can be hundreds of thousands of dollars on the sale price.

Agents who are skilled negotiators devote their lives to studying negotiation. It shows in their results. Yes, they often cost more, but only if they get more. The best agents do not charge anything until they prove their worth. Until you get the best result.

Selecting an agent who gives the biggest selling quote and offers the lowest commission rate is one of the biggest mistakes sellers make.

# 76 If the agent sells my home for less than they quote, do I pay less commission?

Only if you insist.

Contrary to the Biblical saying, the meek do not get a good deal in real estate. The meek get the worst deals.

Stand up for yourself. If you don't think you got a good deal, especially if you got a lower price than the agent first quoted you, you probably deserve to pay less commission. Don't pay a high fee for a low sale price.

Consider how many hours the agent worked on your home. Divide these hours into the amount of commission the agent expects you to pay. The result will likely be more than $1000 an hour. More than heart specialists.

And for what?

To sit at your home for 30 minutes for three Saturdays? And then bring low offers to you.

Repeat: if you are not happy with the service of an agent, stand up for yourself.

If you are disappointed in an offer and the agent insists that the buyers will not pay any more, you can suggest that you will accept the offer if it is *net* to you. This means the commission must be on top of the offered price. The agent will then have to negotiate for themselves.

Agents try harder when their own money is at stake.

# 77 The agent sold my home quickly. Shouldn't I get a commission discount?

Are you paying the agent for getting you a good price or for making you wait a long time? If an agent already has a buyer who's prepared to pay a huge price, this agent is probably super efficient. Be careful not to punish competent agents. Would you punish a doctor who cured you quickly? Of course not.

### A behind-the-scenes fact

Agents often have buyers waiting for homes. But they extend the selling period because many sellers demand a discount on commission if a home is sold quickly. This is another absurdity of the real estate industry. The longer an agent takes to sell your home, the lower the price you are likely to get. That's when you should demand a discount.

# 78 How do I get an agent to give me a commission discount?

First, be confident that you deserve a discount. Or be genuinely outraged that the agent is asking for a high commission for a small effort — never mind the small price. As the saying goes, if you believe it, you can often achieve it.

Second, always be sure you ask for a discount before the sale becomes unconditional. If you have not obtained a discount before the sale becomes legally binding, you will have little chance of succeeding. It would be like eating a meal at a restaurant, patting your tummy in satisfaction — and then asking for a discount.

Here are five powerful questions and comments you can make to an agent to persuade them to give you a discount on their commission:

1. You expect us to drop our price, so we expect you to drop your commission.
2. We said we would be okay to pay you a high commission if you got us a high price. This hasn't happened.
3. How many hours' work have you done to facilitate this sale? We believe you are asking to be paid at least $5000 per hour. We think that's excessive.
4. The price you have negotiated for us is well below the amount you assured us we could get when we met you.
5. Why do agents always blame the market when they can't get the price they promised? And why is the sale price always lower than the original price quoted?

# 79 When should I negotiate the commission?

You can't possibly know how much commission an agent is worth until you see what they can do. It's performance that counts.

It's impossible to rate agents fairly when you first sign up. You can only rate them once you see the results they achieve for you. Good results and a high price may deserve a higher commission. Poor results and a low price — that's when you push them down on the commission.

Don't try and push them down on their commission *before* they start work. That removes their incentive. Scott Kim is an agent who's happy to be paid only after he performs. Yet if he does a superior job he hopes (expects) to be paid well. But he's quick to add this promise: 'If I can only perform to the low standard of my competitors, it would be unethical to charge you more than they charge you'.

Real estate agent Scott Kim says this to sellers:

> Almost all agents expect sellers to trust them. Yet agents are
> ranked the least trustworthy businesspeople in the nation.
> I believe I'm worthy of your trust so therefore instead of you
> having to trust me, I will take the risk and trust you. Let me
> do my job and then see if I'm worth our commission.

You should write on the agent's Listing Agreement the words that Scott Kim and other trustworthy agents have printed on their agreements: *The agent agrees that the commission is negotiable until the point of sale.*

So, not only does the agent now have a better incentive to do well for you, the agent also knows if they don't do well, they don't get paid as well.

Some agents try a terrible bluff by saying that the commission printed on their Listing Agreement cannot be reduced. That's nonsense. Real estate commissions are always negotiable no matter what agents tell you.

What could be fairer than to see how an agent negotiates on your behalf and then decide on the amount of their commission?

# 80 Must I pay for advertising *plus* commission?

No.

Only inexperienced and ill-informed sellers — who have not found an honest and competent agent — pay advertising money *plus* commission.

Agents often spin the sophistry that paying for advertising is 'compulsory'. That's nonsense. Stand up for yourself. Tell all agents that you will only pay commission (and any reasonable expenses) upon the sale of your home. That's when you're happy with the result and the service.

An agent who will not accept such a reasonable condition is not the right agent.

# 81 Do agents get a higher commission for a higher sale price?

Yes, it's true. Agents do get (a little) more commission if they sell a house for more. However, this does not mean agents try harder to get the highest price.

On the contrary.

Real estate commissions are skewed in the wrong direction. There is no incentive for an agent to get an extra $10 000 for a seller when they only get another $200 for themselves and they are already assured of being paid $20 000.

Here's the problem: whether agents sell your home for a higher price or a lower price they still get a high commission.

Further, many agents are so terrified of losing a sale (as their negotiation skills are so poor), they often urge the sellers to accept an offer well below the price the buyers are willing to pay. This is what happens with most sales. While agents are aware of it, most sellers are completely unaware that their homes have been short-sold.

Remember: it doesn't matter how much you once paid for your home, if you don't get the highest market price when you are selling it, you have missed out on money you should have received. Call it 'missing out' or call it a 'loss'. It is the same thing.

That's why it's critical to hire a skilled negotiator.

# 82 Could I be forced to pay double commission?

If you sign up with a second agent without dismissing the first agent, you could be liable for double commission.

If you are involved in negotiations with one agent regarding a specific buyer and you go to another agent who negotiates with the same buyer who then buys your home, you could be liable for double commission.

As mentioned in question 67, if an agent introduces a buyer and then a second agent sells to that same buyer at a later date, you could be liable for double commission.

To avoid paying two commissions to two different agents (for the same home) make sure you only sign up with one agent. Further, if you cross out the nasty clauses found in most standard Listing Agreements — especially clauses about double commissions — you should be safe.

Never sign up with a second agent without getting independent legal advice.

# 83 Is it a mistake to shop around looking for the cheapest commission rate?

Your number one concern when selling a property is the amount you receive in your hand, after expenses. Stop worrying too much — especially in the beginning — about how much commission the agent may get. Start worrying about the final price you're likely to get.

As we saw in question 72, it's vitally important to remember that all commission is negotiable right up until the point of sale. So, however much commission the agent wants, make it clear that you will not make a final decision on the amount of the commission until you have seen the agent's performance and, more importantly, seen the final selling price.

# 84 Can a higher commission really get me a higher sale price?

Only if you have the best agent.

### It's all in the numbers

When Frank listed his home in the Melbourne suburb of Kew, he talked the agent into accepting 1.25 per cent. But then Frank realised that his home was being sold by public auction, which meant a lower sale price. Frank fired the auction agent and hired a skilled negotiator.

Frank was told by the auction agent to expect $2.2 million to $2.4 million. Frank was hoping for $2.8 million. When the skilled negotiator took over the sale of Frank's home, he found several buyers and negotiated with each buyer in private. Frank's home sold for $3.165 million. That was almost $1 million dollars more than the first agent quoted. It was also $365000 above Frank's 'wildest dream price' of $2.8 million.

And the commission charged by the second agent? It was 2.75 per cent.

Frank paid an extra 1.5 per cent in commission to sell his home for an extra 43 per cent.

The final word on commission discounts is this: the best agents get the best prices. They are worth the best commission rate. In all other cases, expect — no, demand — a discount.

# 85 What is a bonus fee — and how does it work?

A bonus fee is a much higher percentage commission paid by sellers if an agent sells their home for a higher price than the agent quoted. And a lower commission if the home sells for its basic price — which is not necessarily a low price.

This is how it is supposed to work...

Let's say the agent and the sellers agree that a home is worth around $2 million: that's its basic price. If the agent sells the home for more than $2 million, the agent will receive a bonus fee (a higher percentage commission for every dollar above $2 million).

The bonus fee is usually between 10 per cent and 30 per cent of the amount above the agent's original quote price (*not* of the entire selling price). Some agents ask for half — yes, 50 per cent — of the amount over the agent's original quote price. That's obscene.

In return for the chance to prove their negotiating skills, the agent will charge a much lower percentage commission on the basic price — in the example, that's a price of $2 million. Instead of charging upwards of 2 per cent, the agent may charge 1 per cent (or less) on the basic price.

This supposedly gives the agent a powerful incentive to get the highest price. And it punishes the agent if they can't get a high price.

Without the bonus fee method, if the agent charged their standard fee of 2 per cent and the home sold for $2 million, the agent would receive a commission of $40 000.

But with the bonus fee method, if the agent charged 1 per cent up to $2 million and 25 per cent on every dollar above $2 million, here are three alternative sale results:

1. If the home sold for $2 million, the agent would get a commission of $20 000 — meaning the sellers would save $20 000 on the usual fee (of $40 000 at 2 per cent).
2. If the home sold for $2.2 million, the agent would get $20 000 on the price of $2 million. But on the extra $200 000, the agent would be paid 25 per cent, which is an extra $50 000. This would give the agent a total commission of $70 000 for a sale of $2.2 million.

3. If the home sold for $2.5 million, the agent would still get $20 000 on the price up to $2 million. However, on the extra $500 000, the agent would get 25 per cent, which is a bonus fee of an extra $125 000. This is a total commission of $145 000 for a sale of $2.5 million.

## The advantage for agents

Using the above example and assuming that the agent would normally be paid 2 per cent, at a sale price of $2.2 million, the agent would receive $26 000 extra commission if they are receiving a bonus fee. Or, if the sale price reached $2.5 million, the agent would receive an extra commission with a bonus fee of $95 000.

## The disadvantage for agents

The above scenario is a substantial risk for the agent. Most agents don't like taking risks. They like to pass the risk on to the sellers.

The risk for the agent is that if the basic market value is $2 million and the agent doesn't have the negotiating skills to get more, then their commission will be cut in half. They will get $20 000 instead of $40 000.

*Beware:* With the bonus fee, some agents want it both ways. They won't discount their commission (under the basic market price) but they will want a bonus fee if they get above the basic market price. Always reject such a scenario.

## The advantage for sellers

The sellers receive $150 000 extra if the sale price of their home is $2.2 million.

At $2.5 million, the sellers receive an extra $375 000.

Sure, the agent gets extremely well paid at these price levels as the bonus fee creates an extraordinarily high commission rate.

But many sellers rightly focus on their own pocket before they focus on the agent's pocket. To them, the extra price is worth the extra commission.

# 86 Are there any catches with bonus fees?

The biggest catch with bonus fees is this: if a home is worth, say, $2.5 million, and the owners — who might be elderly or inexperienced — think their home is only worth about $2 million, the agent can get a bonus they do not deserve. This is why it is so important to get opinions from three different agents as well as doing your own research. And investing in a sworn valuation. Don't pay a bonus fee unless it's well deserved. Unscrupulous agents call the bonus fee 'kicker commission'.

Make sure you're not kicked.

# 87 Are there other costs on top of the commission?

In most cases, yes. Most home sellers face three different costs when selling most homes.

Although, again in most cases, there should only be one cost: commission.

The other two costs are, first, needless marketing costs. This is where most agents rip off many sellers using a system called VPA (vendor paid advertising). It's not unusual for sellers to be hit with $5000 in marketing costs (more on high-end homes). This cost is payable even if a home is not sold. In such cases, agents profit from the sellers' losses. As do real estate websites. For more on VPA, see question 134.

The other unnecessary cost is usually far more detrimental than either commission or marketing. It's also a cost that most home sellers are never aware of. This is the short-sell cost. In most cases, homes are short-sold because the agents focus on the lowest price sellers will accept instead of the highest price buyers will pay. Incredibly, while most agents are good at pushing sellers down in price, few know how to push buyers up in price.

The average cost of the short-sell is 10 per cent of the final selling price. So, if a home sells for $2 million, it probably should have sold for $2.2 million. That's a $200 000 cost that's often hidden, all because some agents are too ignorant or too unethical to learn the skill of negotiating.

Out of these three costs, you should usually only pay for one: a commission. And only once your home has been sold at a price at which you are happy. But to only pay one cost, you'll need to stand up for yourself.

# 88 What are the different fees some agents try to charge?

Beware of costs such as the following.

- *Advertising fees.* Many agents have a minimum charge of several thousand dollars (at least $5000) for advertising, regardless of whether or not advertising is needed. Also, the higher the median price of homes in your area, the higher the cost of advertising. Reject agents who have mandatory advertising fees (which are applicable even if they fail to sell your home).

- *Administration fee.* This can be as high as $500.
- *Auctioneer's fee.* This can reach $1000 and is always payable, even if your home is sold by private treaty before the scheduled auction, and therefore there was no auction.
- *Copywriting fee.* It can cost as much as $500 to write the advertisement for your home — no matter how badly it's written.
- *Professional photography fee.* This will be at least several hundred dollars. You'd be better off using your phone to take three or four reasonable (but honest) shots.
- *Video fee.* This can add another $1000 or more so that sellers think they are getting a better service.
- *Translation fee.* Yes, some agents have been known to charge hundreds of dollars to translate the advertisement for your home into a foreign language. Google does it for nothing.
- *Legal fees.* If you refuse to abide by the Listing Agreement (no matter how unconscionable), many agents will employ lawyers to threaten you. You will be charged for this 'service'.
- *Open for inspection fee.* Some agents charge you for the privilege of sitting at your home for 30 minutes waiting for buyers to show up — whereupon they will also charge you thousands of dollars if a buyer falls in love with your home and wants to buy it.
- *Social media fee.* You could be charged for the cost of the agent's social media consultant.
- *Drone fee.* This is another fee often payable to the agent's mate, who got a drone as a birthday present.
- *Signboard fee.* You'll pay as much as $2000 for a sign — usually with a glamour shot of the agent.
- *Caveat lodgement fee.* If you refuse to pay some fees — whether unfair or not — you could have a caveat lodged on your home. For this you will be charged a fee. When the caveat is

discharged (once the agent is satisfied that you have paid your debt to them) you will be charged a discharge fee.

- *Double commission fee.* If you inadvertently sign up with two agents, both could claim commission from you even though only one agent sold your home.
- *Floorplan.* This could cost between $80 and $200.



# 89 What is the fairest commission rate — for agents and owners?

It can't be stated too often: the most important word when considering commission is *justification*.

The agent should be able to get enough on the selling price to easily cover their commission. Otherwise, why pay them — especially when, as you will see, in many cases sellers could sell their own homes and get the same or a better result.

There should be no objection by any fair-minded person to an agent earning $40 000 for selling a home for, say, $2.3 million if the agent's negotiating skills have been responsible for the price increasing by, say, $200 000 or $300 000.

But if a home sells for $2 million and dozens of buyers would have paid that price or more, the sellers would have been better off sticking a sign on their lawn and dealing with door knockers.

So, a fair commission for selling a home where the agent has done nothing to obtain a selling price to cover their commission is nothing.

If, however, an agent sells a home and more than covers their commission, they are entitled to be paid well. Perhaps even congratulated.

## Paying high commission can be worth it

I once paid 5 per cent commission to a Brisbane agent who managed to sell some hard-to-sell properties for more than local agents estimated.

## Key takeaways from part 4

▸ The most important word related to commission is *justify*. Has the agent more than paid for themselves *or* have they done nothing that you could not have done yourself?

▸ There are three costs in selling a home; first, the commission; second, the amount by which a home is short-sold (as with most homes); and third, needless marketing costs.

▸ The average commission in Australia is 2 per cent. In New Zealand it's close to 4 per cent.

▸ Many agents are obsessed with GCI: gross commission income.

- Most agents expend fewer than 10 hours of actual work to sell a home.
- If an agent wants you to sell for less than they quoted, offer them less commission.
- Sometimes, paying a higher commission can lead to a higher price and a fast sale. In such cases the agent may deserve a good rate of commission.
- You can offer a bonus commission if your house sells for a higher price. But make sure you know the value of your home first so you're not paying a bonus for simply getting market value. Get legal advice.
- Real estate commission is *always* negotiable until the point of sale.
- Only negotiate the commission after you see how the agent performs.
- You do *not* have to pay for commission *and* advertising.
- Only naïve and inexperienced sellers pay marketing costs before a sale.
- Be careful of hidden fees. Read the fine print before signing up.
- Be sure that the commission you pay is fair and justified.
- Never pay any money until your home is sold and you are happy with the price.

# PART 5

# DECIDING ON A SELLING METHOD

Of everything you read in this book—and all the questions and answers you need to know—nothing is more important than the method you choose to sell your home.

The wrong method can cost you tens—even hundreds—of thousands of dollars in underselling your home. On high-end homes, sellers can lose millions of dollars if they use the wrong method.

And here's the irony: most sellers who choose the wrong method of sale never know what happened. Some even thank agents for underselling their homes: little do they know by how much they were undersold.

In this part, you will learn that many common methods might be good for agents, but they are not so good for sellers.

Please realise that you and most agents have different agendas. Your agenda is to sell your home for the best possible price. The agenda of most agents is to sell your home at any price.

By the time you have finished reading part 5 of this book, you will have the knowledge to insist that your home is sold in the manner that gets the best market price. You will also know how to resist the slick lines that many agents use to manipulate you into using a method that's best for the agents.

## Questions in this part

90. What is the best selling method?
91. What is an 'off-market' sale?
92. Is 'expression of interest' a good way to sell?
93. What's so great about expressions of interest?
94. Isn't transparency supposed to be honest and ethical?
95. Why don't more agents sell by expression of interest?
96. Is auction a good way to sell?
97. As many homes in my area are auctioned, shouldn't I sell by auction too?
98. If auctions are bad for sellers why do so many sell by auction?
99. Don't auctions attract buyers?
100. Do dummy bids and dummy offers still exist?
101. Surely the reserve price protects me from underselling?
102. What are auction clearance rates and are they accurate?
103. Why do many sellers seem happy after an auction?
104. Why are most auctioneers male?
105. What is a silent auction and can it get the best price?

# 90 What is the best selling method?

The best method of selling is the one that gets you the best price. And that method is to sell respectfully and fairly by private negotiation.

Beware of the cliché, 'There is no one-size-fits-all method', that some agents use to justify flawed methods such as public auction. This is ridiculous. Some agents want to be all things to all people. They will recommend a method regardless of whether it is ethical or in the best interests of sellers.

But there *is* a selling method suitable for *all* properties and all sellers. It's a method that eschews any method not in the sellers' best interests, such as auction or multi-listing or (usually) a general listing.

And this is the method: *the best agents discover the best price the best buyers will pay. And this is always best done by private negotiation. That's the best selling method if you want the best price with the least stress.*

This method enables agents to qualify buyers and discover their highest price. (Qualifying buyers is explained in question 162.) Agents can't get the highest price for a home unless they know the highest price buyers are prepared to pay.

# 91 What is an 'off-market' sale?

If this question is answered truthfully, it may seem hard to believe. At least, at first.

But here goes, in two words: *better price.* Yes, believe it. In many (if not most) cases, you will get a better price if you find an agent with the integrity and skill to do an off-market sale.

Actually, the term 'off-market' is misleading. It implies that you don't go *in* the market. That's not true. It's what critics, dodgy agents and website ad pushers — and all those who benefit from massive advertising — want you to believe.

Here's why you are likely to get a better price off-market. The best paying buyers, as mentioned, are those who fall in love with your home; those who feel it's special; and, most of all, those who get in first. These buyers pay a better price. Often as much as 20 to 30 per cent more. That can be hundreds of thousands of dollars for you and your family.

But, if your home is widely promoted (on-market) and doesn't sell, there's a reason. That reason is usually that the price is too high. At least, that's what buyers believe. So, you will be offered a lower price.

When your home is off-market you can get a better price. Because it's unique. It's special. And that inspires buyers to offer their best price before other buyers see it. Unlike on-market homes, which are like stale fruit and sell for bargain prices.

So, the term 'off-market' means that agents should do what agents did years ago — and what the best ones do today. Instead of being lazy (and dishonest) and taking thousands of dollars of your money to advertise to people known to the agents, they should contact those people and sell your home for a better price.

'Off-market' equals better price. That's often the right formula.

# 92 Is 'expression of interest' a good way to sell?

Michael Kies is a former agent. And an honest and brilliant one. In a 12-year sales career, he averaged more sales per month than many salespeople now average in a year. Most of his business (sellers and buyers) came from referrals. Michael's real estate life was dedicated to getting the best result for sellers. He became one of the world's best real estate negotiators. He also bought several investment properties. Now retired and only involved with real estate as a buyer, this is Michael's five-word comment about expressions of interest (EOI): 'I hate expressions of interest!'

When asked *why* he hates EOI, Michael replied, 'Because it forces me to pay my best price. It's not like public auctions where I can buy for less than I want to pay. With expressions of interest, I must offer my maximum'.

In a nutshell, expressions of interest are terrible for bargain hunters, but great for home sellers.

# 93 What's so great about expressions of interest?

With expressions of interest, interested buyers make their offers in confidence. Unlike public auctions, where all buyers see what other buyers are offering — and therefore only have to offer a small amount above the buyer below them — expressions of interest are private. It's like a tender process without the absurdity of transparency, which ruins the seller's chance of getting the highest price.

The great benefit of EOI is a higher price for the sellers.

# 94 Isn't transparency supposed to be honest and ethical?

Many agents love to describe their methods, or even themselves, as totally transparent. But being transparent with everything works against the interests of the sellers.

One of the worst things for sellers is an agent who discloses the amount of all offers to each buyer. This ruins the chance of the sellers getting the best price.

So often, when buyers ask if they can make an offer, the agent will reveal the details of any current offers. For example, if a home is priced at $3 million and buyers want to make an offer — but have yet to state their amount — the agent may reply, 'We've already got an offer of $2.7 million'. The buyers, who may well have been prepared to pay $2.9 million, now decide to offer $2.75 million, which is $50 000 more than the other offer. The agent will get excited and run to the seller and say, 'Hey, I just got you another $50 000 from another buyer'. The inference being, of course, that the agent is a hot negotiator.

But no, the agent is actually an incompetent negotiator because the agent persuaded the sellers to accept $2.75 million from buyers who — unbeknown to the agent — were willing to offer $2.9 million. So, instead of getting 'an extra $50 000' as the sellers and the incompetent agent believe, the sellers have short-sold by $150 000. All because the agent was 'transparent'.

Imagine this behaviour with a government tender process: a large project where competing builders (like competing buyers in real estate) must tender to win the rights to construct a project.

And imagine if one builder persuaded a government employee to disclose the amounts tendered by other builders. The consequences of disclosing other tenders could lead to a jail sentence for the employee (and the builder).

Yet, many real estate agents do the same thing constantly (especially at auctions) and then act as if they are ethical because they are 'transparent'.

It shouldn't be called transparency. It's absurdity. And it's a huge breach of the confidentiality needed to protect the interests of the home sellers, who are paying the agent's commission.

# 95 Why don't more agents sell by expression of interest?

The reason most agents don't use expressions of interest is because it involves two words that are anathema to many agents: hard work.

Instead of spending 15 to 20 minutes yelling at buyers at auctions, with expressions of interest the agents must speak privately with each buyer. This is how skilled negotiators get the best price: by sitting with buyers and qualifying them (see question 162). Buyers appreciate an agent who takes time to consider their needs.

But each buyer will require at least an hour of the agent's time, perhaps two or three hours. If there are six buyers interested in a home, the agent will need to work between six and 18 hours — a lot longer than 15 or 20 minutes at an auction. Plus travelling time to visit each buyer.

Therefore, the total time spent negotiating with expressions of interest could easily be 20 hours, whereas an auction only takes about 20 minutes (if it can even be called 'negotiating'). The way agents see it, they must work 60 times as hard to earn the same money if they use private negotiation.

Even if the home sold for more by EOI — let's say $2 200 000 instead of $2 000 000 at auction (which is about the average the sellers would get if they chose private negotiation instead of public auction) — the agent's commission may rise to $44 000. That's only an extra $4000 for doing 60 times the negotiating work.

# 96 Is auction a good way to sell?

For a seller, auction is the worst way to sell any home. In any area. At any time. The reason is simple: with a public auction, it's impossible to be assured of selling for the highest price. Most homes at auctions are sold for tens — even hundreds — of thousands of dollars below their highest price. High-end homes can undersell by millions of dollars.

Agents who claim that a public auction is the best way to sell property are not acting in the best interests of home sellers. There can be no other explanation for foisting such an ancient, flawed and unsuitable method upon sellers, most of whom never know their homes are undersold.

Plus, auctions incur needless expenses that enrich the agents and their acolytes (all of whom spread the myth that auctions are the best way to sell properties). There is not a single so-called benefit with an auction that cannot be bettered by selling using superior methods.

Auctions are stressful. Sellers are often pressured into making life-changing decisions in seconds during the manipulated high-pressure atmosphere of an auction. Such stress prevents sellers from thinking clearly. As one industry training manual teaches agents about auctions: 'Move quickly. They are usually numb. Don't give them time to dwell on the price'.

Agents like auctions because auctions are best for agents. Auctions give agents more money for less work.

> *Auctions enable agents to condition sellers down in price and therefore make sales faster and get their commission sooner.*

As the Real Estate Institute teaches agents, 'Auction is the fastest and best conditioning method'.

Let me say it again: auction is the worst method for selling a home. Any home. In any area. At any time.

> ## Never sell at auction
>
> Some agents will claim that I sold one of my own properties at auction. These agents are mistaken. I have never sold any property at auction. I have, however, bought many properties at auction and re-sold them (often immediately) by private negotiation for thousands of dollars more. Sometimes near double the price paid at auction.

# 97 As many homes in my area are auctioned, shouldn't I sell by auction too?

It doesn't matter if everyone else in your area seems to be selling by auction — don't do it.

The only people who sell by auction are those who don't understand how homes are undersold at auction or those who want to sell quickly for a cheap price.

If most people in an area auction their homes, here's the truth: most sellers in that area waste thousands of dollars on needless expenses. Worse, they undersell their homes. Most never realise what happens at auctions. Just because a road is well travelled doesn't mean it's the right road.

Buyers don't buy a home because it's auctioned. Buyers buy a home because they like the home.

Research shows that most buyers dislike auctions. If you reject going to auction, you will attract more genuine buyers and usually get a better price.

# 98 If auctions are bad for sellers why do so many sell by auction?

Because many agents persuade homeowners that auction is the best way to get the best price. The reality is the opposite. Auctions are best for agents. Not home sellers.

# 99 Don't auctions attract buyers?

No, they attract crowds. There are more neighbours, stickybeaks and agents at auctions than buyers. Auctions repel more buyers than they attract.

Buyers are not attracted to homes because homes are offered for sale by auction. Buyers are attracted because they like the homes.

All agents receive comments from some buyers saying, 'We are not interested in homes for auction'. But no agent meets buyers who refuse to negotiate privately and confidentially.

The reason there are often large crowds at auctions is because so many agents underquote the likely selling price to buyers. Agents do everything from blatant underquoting in the advertising to their nudge-nudge, wink-wink inferences such as, 'This could go cheap'.

And so, at any auction there will be a crowd of salivating buyers hoping to bag your home for a bargain price. If you refuse to lower your reserve price to the disappointingly low amount offered by bargain-seeking bidders, the agent will say, 'This is what the market is telling you'. To which you should reply, 'No, this is because you deceived bargain hunters about the price of our home'.

Auctions are the domain of vulture buyers. As a homeowner, your primary duty is to protect the value of your home.

A sale by auction — like excessive advertising — damages your home's value.

# 100 Do dummy bids and dummy offers still exist?

Yes, they sure do.

### Dummy bids

Dummy bids still happen at auctions. Even though buyers must register and be given a 'paddle number' (in some states), dummy bids are not extinct (as some agents claim).

As many agents laughingly comment, they 'just get dummy bidders to register'. The purpose of dummy bidding, however, is not to give extra money to a seller — it's to give momentum to an auction.

If there is only one bidder, an auction becomes a farce. Dummy bidders are to auctions what spark plugs are to engines.

### Dummy offers

The purpose of a dummy offer is to condition sellers to lower their prices. These offers are setting the sellers up for the genuine offers that follow the dummy offers. Dummy offers are well below the price wanted by the seller. This ensures an agent will not get caught out if the sellers accept the dummy offer. An agent knows there is no risk of the seller accepting the fictitious offer.

The purpose of dummy offers is to make real offers look good.

# 101 Surely the reserve price protects me from underselling?

If an agent says that your reserve price at auction protects you from underselling your home, who protects you from those agents? Who protects you from their relentless conditioning to convince you to lower your price and grind you down? Many home sellers compare conditioning with psychological torture. They become such nervous wrecks that they'll do almost anything to relieve the stress. They crack and sell at any price. And that's exactly what so many agents want — a sale at any price.

There is a well-known saying about life: 'You get what you focus upon'. Auctions focus on the lowest price.

You see, once the agents know your lowest price (called the 'reserve'), they will focus on nothing else. They will underquote your likely reserve price to buyers. If you get alarmed, the agent will attempt to assuage your fears with a common (and stupidly deceptive) statement: 'I have been doing this for years. Trust me. Promoting a lower price will attract more buyers; then we talk them up in price'.

Nonsense.

By promoting too low a price you attract more buyers, sure. But at a lower price. In the heat of the live auction, the agent will insist this is 'what the market is telling you'. It's not. This low price is what the agent has told buyers.

If you think your reserve price protects you from underselling your home, think again. Nothing will protect you from agents bullying you to undersell your home.

# 102 What are auction clearance rates and are they accurate?

Auction clearance rates are dodgy. Always have been and probably always will be. They measure the percentage of properties sold at auction over a specific period and are deliberately distorted to make auctions seem successful.

To get an accurate reading of the auction clearance rates, you'll have to basically halve the published figures. For example, if there are 100 properties offered for sale by auction and only 30 are sold, the publicly released clearance rate will be around 60 per cent. But, of course, you know it's 30 per cent.

Fake auction clearance rates are released every week in all states. Such blatant deception has been happening for years. In one absurd case (in Perth), 12 properties were offered for auction and none sold at auction. The claimed clearance rate was 30 per cent.

Here's a brief explanation of how auction clearance rates are faked:

- Agents include properties sold by private negotiation as sales made by auction.
- Agents exclude properties that fail to sell at auction. These are listed as 'unreported'.
- Agents base their success rate on skewed figures that appear legitimate to outsiders.

Let's say 1000 homes are scheduled for auction. And let's say 200 of those homes sell by private negotiation *before* the auction. And let's say that another 300 homes are sold by private negotiation *after* the auction. That's 500 homes that did *not* sell *at* auction. But they are all counted as sales by auction. Of the other 500 homes, let's say only 200 sell *at* auction.

In truth, therefore, of the 1000 homes scheduled for auction, only 200 actually sold *at* the auction. As any school child will attest, 200 sales from 1000 auctions is a 20 per cent clearance rate.

But not if these children grow up to be auction agents.

Here's how the industry calculates auction clearance rates: 1000 properties are put to auction. Five hundred of those properties sell *before* or *after* the auction but only 200 properties sell *at* the auction. That's a total of 700 sales.

So, the industry now creates the false impression that all 700 homes sold *at* auction.

And so, they issue a fake clearance rate of 70 per cent. In other words, a 20 per cent clearance rate magically becomes a 70 per cent clearance rate.

# 103 Why do many sellers seem happy after an auction?

Because they have been gaslighted and duped. These sellers are like cuckolds who don't know they're cuckolds.

This especially applies when sellers get a higher price than they expect. Some thank the agent. Yes, for underselling their homes!

Ignorance can be horrendously costly. As con artists know, the best cons are where the marks (victims) don't know they are being conned.

The final focus should not be the amount of the selling price. It should be the amount the buyers were prepared to pay.

If the buyers have not paid their highest price, the property has been undersold.

This happens at most auctions.

# 104 Why are most auctioneers male?

Auctions are perfect for show-pony males. Men with massive egos who love to be the centre of attention — albeit for a few minutes. Such men relish the power, especially when several buyers are bidding. Their chests swell like male peacocks.

But surely some women like attention?

Well yes, but there is an aspect of auctions that women generally find repulsive: bullying.

Just go to any in-room auction with any network and you will likely witness bullying akin to domestic violence. Terrified home sellers — often elderly people — are harangued and shamed into underselling their homes.

As we approach the 2030s, most agents will soon be women. And yet, less than 10 per cent of auctioneers are women.

Women are usually kinder than men.

# 105 What is a silent auction and can it get the best price?

A silent, or private, auction is a much smarter and far superior way of selling than a public auction. With a silent auction, none of the buyers know the amount offered by the other buyers. This enables the owners to get a higher price — often the highest price — especially if the agent is a skilled negotiator. Buyers are compelled to offer their best price rather than just one increment above the bidder below them because, unlike public auctions, the bids at a silent auction are private. They are only known to the agent and the seller. This is why a silent auction is sometimes called a private auction.

In just one example, a farmer had listed his cattle station for public auction. Then he researched auctions and discovered how they cause most properties to be undersold. He cancelled the public auction and instructed the agent to use a silent auction. The property sold for $7 million more than if it had been sold at a public auction.

So yes, a silent auction is far superior to a public auction. Indeed, it's the opposite. At a public auction you often get the lowest price. At a silent auction you get the highest price.

The challenge for sellers is finding an agent prepared to conduct a silent auction. Most agents don't like this method because — as with expressions of interest — it involves more work.

## Key takeaways from part 5

▸ To get the best price for your home, choose the best method. This means discovering the highest price buyers will pay.

▸ An off-market sale can get the best price — if you hire a great agent.

▸ Expressions of interest (EOI) discover a buyer's highest price.

▸ The reason more agents don't use EOI is because it's more work for them.

▸ Beware of the word 'transparency'. It can cause your home to be massively undersold.

▸ The public auction method is the worst way to sell any home in any area. That's why I have never sold any of my own homes by public auction.

▸ The reserve price does not protect you. It causes you to undersell.

▸ Auction clearance rates are inaccurate. Always have been, always will be.

▸ The reason sellers seem happy after their homes are auctioned is because they have focused on the amount by which their home sold *above reserve* rather than the amount their home has sold *below the buyers' highest price.*

▸ A silent (or private) auction is an excellent way to achieve the highest price.

# PART 6

# PRICING YOUR HOME FOR A SUCCESSFUL SALE

In this part, you will discover that you need to focus on two important factors when pricing your home. First, you need to be sure you achieve the best price. And second, you need to be sure that you protect the value of your home.

You will need a pricing strategy that does not attract low-paying buyers who will then give you lower offers than you expect. All agents know that the lower the price of a home, the easier it is to sell the home — and the faster the agents earn their commission. Anyone can sell any home if the price is low enough: that takes no skill or effort.

Don't be lured into using a strategy that attracts buyers by creating the impression that they can buy at a lower price.

To protect your home's value and achieve the right price, the first thing you need to do is attract a buyer who can pay the right price.

The questions and answers in part 6 will guide you towards pricing your home for success.

# Questions in this part

# 106 How do I know what price to ask?

Probably the most common mistake made by home sellers is overestimating the value of their homes. It doesn't matter how much you love your home or how highly you value it, what matters is how much buyers love it.

The minute you enter the real estate market you are in competition with other homes. So, unless you are in the rare position of having an uncommonly unique home, you must face the fact that your home is worth what other similar ones in the area are worth.

This doesn't mean you can't get a better price than other similar homes, especially when you understand how most homes are undersold.

As hard as it may be, try to be objective and consider two factors with regard to pricing.

## *Price too high, sell too low*

Many sellers ask so much money for their homes that buyers shun their home. Pretty soon, overpriced homes become lemons. And there is only one way to sell unwanted homes: drop the price.

If you start too high — or worse, if you stubbornly hold out for an unrealistically high price — you will almost certainly end up selling too low. Or withdrawing from sale.

## *A lower asking price can mean a higher selling price*

You are better off asking too little than too much. Why? Because if your home is slightly underpriced you will almost certainly attract multiple buyers. This can lead to multiple offers, which can easily see your home sell above its market price — provided your agent is a skilled negotiator. This is how many homes are sold in the United States.

*Please note:* Never advertise a price that you would never consider yourself. That's bait pricing, which is illegal.

Here are three ways to get a good idea of what price to ask for your home:

1. Call in two, three or four agents (no more) and ask them how much they believe your home is worth. Make it clear that you have no intention of choosing the agent who gives you the highest quote. Once you have received three or four different prices you will have some idea of the price you should be asking. Remember, however, agents tend to overquote because they are keen to win your listing.

2. A valuation can be an excellent investment. Valuers have no hidden agendas. You pay them a fee, and they quote you a value. Generally, most valuers are more accurate and honest than many agents. If you don't like the valuation, you don't have to share it with anybody. It's confidential.

3. Be careful comparing your home with the prices of homes that have been sold. Given that most (about 90 per cent) of homes are undersold, you will be comparing your home with undersold ones. To get a more accurate guide to the likely price of your home, add at least 10 per cent to the sale price of comparable homes.

# 107 Should I pay for a valuation from a registered valuer?

Yes, it's always a good idea to contact a valuer before you contact an agent. Unless, of course, you are confident about the true value of your property. But, even then, the cost of a valuation — which is minor compared to the value of your property — is likely worth it.

> *Valuers have been described as the 'hidden heroes of real estate'.*

Sure, they are not perfect and sometimes sellers (and buyers) disagree with their valuations. But they are a lot closer to perfect than the average agent. And they are usually honest.

# 108 What does 'protecting the value' of a home mean?

Protecting the value of a home means exactly what it says. You look after the value of your home the same way you look after the value of anything you own. You maintain it well; you present it well — especially when you are selling. You focus on what protects the value. And you avoid anything that damages the value.

No homeowner deliberately damages the value of their home. But few realise how much damage is caused when selling — especially if that home spends too much time on the market.

Those internet ads might be great for the profile of agents, but they often disclose too much information. People who are not interested in a home, or who are not likely to buy it, start talking about it — especially locals. This includes other agents, many of whom will make negative comments. Agents delight in the phrase, 'Oh, that place has been for sale forever'. Without any prompting, they make derisory comments such as, 'It's just overpriced; that's what's wrong with it'. Spreading the word that a listing is overpriced damages its value.

Perhaps the worst way that homes are damaged in value is with auctions.

> *Most homes offered for auction fail to sell at the auction.*

And a sale does not mean that a home sold for the best market price. At auctions most homes are short-sold.

Consider this: the word 'clearance' (when applied to sales) means cheap. Always has done. So, when agents talk about successful clearance rates at auctions all they mean is that they made lots of sales. This is what happens at retail outlets like Supercheap Auto. Prices are low because of high and fast turnover. Great for buyers. But not so great for sellers in real estate.

From the moment their homes carry the word 'auction', their value is damaged. Property auctions should be called Supercheap Real Estate.

# 109 What is a 'heart buyer'?

Heart buyers are buyers who fall in love with a home. Like lovers who desperately yearn for each other, heart buyers will do almost anything to buy a home they love.

If you are fortunate enough to have a heart buyer fall in love with your home, you will almost certainly get a fantastic price — if your agent is a competent negotiator.

It also helps if you have a lovable home, just as being a lovable person helps you find (and keep) a loving partner. Don't get your hopes up, however, because if you haven't got a competent agent, you're unlikely to get a heart price.

So, just as you would do if you were going on a romantic date, get your home looking its best. And then hire the best agent.

# 110 Does a lower price attract more buyers?

A lower price attracts more buyers. But you have to be careful not to go so low that you break the law or attract buyers who can only afford the lower price. It's better to say that an *attractive* price will attract more buyers. But be warned: an unrealistic price repels buyers.

Setting an attractive asking price will attract genuine buyers. If you're allowed to use a price range in your state, be sure that you're happy to sell anywhere within that range. Make sure that your agent (or you) makes it clear to all prospective buyers that if there are multiple buyers, each buyer will be asked to make their best offer. With private negotiation, there isn't the high pressure that comes with an auction. This will not only attract more buyers; it will ensure that the best buyers offer their best price. And you, the owner, will be able to accept the most attractive offer without being under pressure.

# 111 Should I ask a high price and negotiate rather than sell low by asking a low price?

Some sellers place too much importance on the asking price of their homes. Remember, an asking price is exactly that: an *asking* price. It is not the final selling price, which could be higher or lower than the asking price.

Here's how to know if your pricing is right or wrong: if your price is too high, you'll get no interest or low interest. If your price is too low, you'll get high interest.

The fear of selling too low will not bother you if you understand real estate negotiation. Multiple potential buyers for your home can mean multiple offers.

And with private negotiation — unlike public auction — none of the buyers know what other buyers are offering. This forces them to offer their highest price rather than try and snipe you for a lower price.

# 112 What is 'bait pricing'?

Bait pricing is deliberately promoting a property well below its value and below what the seller will accept. Bait pricing is illegal.

The first rule with doing business in real estate should be 'obey the law'. And remember, there are two laws. First, the legal law. And second, the moral law.

Do the right thing legally, do the right thing ethically, and you'll get a better result. You'll feel better too.

# 113 What is a hidden search price and how can it hurt me?

A home's hidden search price is the price at which the home appears in the search results of a major real estate website. This hidden price is chosen and set by the agent when uploading the home and its details to the website.

A hidden search price controls which buyers see your home. This is good in theory; however, some agents use the hidden search price to convince sellers to lower their asking prices. It becomes part of the agent's conditioning strategy on the sellers. It could be described as pseudo bait pricing.

For example, if you are trying to sell your home for $2 million, the agent may set the hidden search price at $1.7 million. This means that all the buyers who discover your home online will have searched around $1.7 million. Your home would not appear for buyers searching for properties at $2 million or more (the price you want).

If your home is for sale with an agent now, here's how you can discover the hidden search price that your agent has set for your home:

1. Go to the website where your home is advertised.
2. Search for homes matching your home (exact bedrooms, bathrooms, land size, etc.).
3. Set the filter for a maximum price above your home's value. For example, for a home worth about $2 million, set a maximum price of $2.5 million on the filter (with no minimum price on the filter).
4. Continue entering a lower maximum price (by small increments) until your home no longer appears in the search results.

The last price at which your home appears is the hidden price set by the agent.

So, if a $2 million home stops appearing at $1.6 million, this means that your agent has set the hidden search price for your home somewhere between $1.6 million and $1.7 million.

If your agent is telling you that buyer interest ('the market') for your home is coming in at $1.6 million to $1.7 million, that's because the agent has set the hidden search price in that range.

So, if you want $2 million for your home and the agent (in the above example) tells you that there is 'no interest for your home at $2 million' that's because the agent has set the hidden search prices lower than $2 million. Buyers who may pay $2 million for your home need to be able to find your home.

A hidden search price at an amount below the price wanted by the sellers is a clever (but sneaky) way for agents to convince the sellers to lower their price expectations.

The lower the price, the easier a home is to sell.

And, of course, the lower the price quoted to attract buyers, the more buyers are attracted. This often descends into bait pricing. The agent may tell the sellers, 'This is what the market is saying'.

But if the agent has been using a low hidden search price, then obviously *the agent has attracted the wrong market.*

If you want to sell your home for $2 million, you need to attract buyers who can afford to pay $2 million.

If your home is currently for sale and you discover that your agent is using a lower hidden search price to condition you to drop your price, you need to drop the agent. Immediately.

# 114 Should I offer my home with or without a displayed price?

Research over many years consistently shows that when homes are advertised without a price, they get less interest. However, in many areas today, most homes are advertised without a price. This is absurd because in a few seconds anyone can get an idea of the value of a home online.

Therefore, it is better to display a price (or even a sensible and honest price range) than to display no price. Your home will stand out. Buyers will appreciate your honesty.

One of the main reasons for not displaying a price is because the price is too high. But buyers are not silly. They realise this fact, which is why many buyers overlook homes without prices.

Be proud of your price. Display it with confidence — if you feel your home is worth it.

# 115 What do I do if the agent is quoting below online estimates?

Sorry to disappoint you, but if the online price is higher than the price given to you by the agent, the agent is likely correct. The agent has seen your home. The agent knows the market in your local area. The internet has never seen your home.

Even though much of the world is falling in love with artificial intelligence, it is a step backward from genuine intelligence.

Agents are generally more accurate with pricing than most internet prices, some of which can be wrong by hundreds of thousands of dollars.

Let high internet quotes make you feel good if you are not selling. But when it comes time to sell, the agent — or, better still, a valuer — is a better source of price accuracy.

# 116 Why do so many owners get the value of their home so wrong?

When most homes come on the market, the owners are expecting too high a price. There are three reasons for this phenomenon:

1.  First, the sellers think their home is better than other people's homes. This is human instinct.
2.  Second, agents have inflated the price to entice sellers to list with their agency.
3.  Third, the sellers are overly optimistic. Few are as greedy as agents claim. There is nothing wrong with being optimistic.

The main problem with overpricing a property is that it becomes stale in the marketplace and eventually sells for less than it could have sold for had it been priced correctly at the start.

A real estate truism is this: *If you start too high, you'll sell too low.* Be careful.

# 117 What is a 'comparable market analysis' and can I trust it?

A comparable market analysis (also known as a CMA) is where agents compare the prices of sold homes with the prices of homes yet to be sold.

Most CMAs are misleading. This is because most homes are undersold by about 10 per cent.

When an agent presents you with a CMA, similar homes to yours have likely been undersold.

Therefore, when you are being presented with a CMA, it's prudent to add 10 per cent to those comparable values.

# 118 How can I know how much my home is worth?

There are six ways that homeowners commonly use to discover the value of their homes:

1. *They visit other homes being sold in their area.* But be careful of auction sales. Despite the carnival appearances, most homes are undersold at auctions.
2. *They check real estate websites.* Be careful to look for *sold* prices. Don't focus on *asking* prices.

3.  *They look at online estimates.* These are unreliable. They usually give you three estimates of the value of your home: lowest price, highest price and likely price (which they call 'high confidence'). Ask them to buy your home at the 'high confidence' price and see what happens. The big trouble with these online price estimates is that the buyers all want to pay the lowest price estimated (which is often far too low) and the sellers all want to receive the highest price estimated (which is often too high). Don't trust this method.

4.  *They call in three agents.* And remember three words: 'Don't sign anything'. Given that many agents inflate the likely sale price, here's a question to ask that's like a real-estate-agent-truth-serum: *What is the price you could absolutely guarantee I'll get assuming that you won't get any commission if you sell below that price?* So, for example, if an agent says that your home is worth 'between $1.7 million and $2 million', will they agree to accept no commission if the best they can sell your home for is less than $1.7 million?

5.  *They pay for a valuer.* Valuers tend to be conservative (they would prefer to say 'careful'). But remember, unlike agents, valuers have no vested interest in inflating the value of your home. (Beware that many agents claim to offer 'free valuations' but in most cases this is an inaccurate or misleading claim as only registered and qualified valuers can provide valuations.)

6.  *They list their home for sale.* Make sure that all the offers are the best offers the buyers are prepared to pay. Your agent must discover their 'walk-away' price. A home is *not* necessarily worth what a buyer will pay. It is worth what a skilled agent can persuade a buyer to pay. The difference can be enormous.

## Key takeaways from part 6

▶ Your home competes with other similar homes for sale.

▶ It is vitally important to protect the value of your home.

▶ At the same time, don't overestimate the value of your home.

▶ If you price your home too high at the start, you will likely sell too low at the end.

▶ A lower (or more reasonable) asking price often gets you a higher selling price.

▶ A 'heart buyer' will often pay you above market price. Be sure your agent knows how to attract and negotiate with potential heart buyers.

▶ No matter how much you may be tempted, never allow bait pricing. It's illegal.

▶ If you suspect too many low offers, check the agent's hidden search price.

▶ Online price estimates are often massively inaccurate. Don't let them fool you.

▶ Beware of CMAs, as most of these comparison homes have likely been undersold.

▶ Be proud of your asking price.

▶ Always remember the six ways to know the value of your home (see question 118).

# PART 7

# PRESENTING YOUR HOME FOR SALE

The best presented homes attract the best paying buyers.

In this part, you'll see how you can present your home at its best. Staging is all the rage in real estate these days. But staging is expensive. Unless you can get a return far in excess of the cost of staging, why do it? Do some research into the different costs needed to spruce up a home. Look for examples where staging (and minor renovations) can increase the value of a home by tens of thousands of dollars.

As well as presenting your home at its best, you need to ensure that you attract genuine and qualified buyers to your home. Hordes of stickybeaks can damage the value of your home.

Once you attract the best buyers, you need to know the most important factors that persuade those buyers to fall in love with your home. One of the best ideas is to prepare a 'love list'. That—and many other ideas in this part—will ensure that you know how to present your home at its absolute best.

# Questions in this part

# 119 What inclusions should I offer with my home?

Don't be too hasty to offer too much too soon. Most buyers will make you an offer below your desired price. If you have included a massive number of inclusions, you deprive yourself of good bargaining chips.

But, if you are only offering fixed inclusions and then you get an offer, instead of lowering your price you can offer extra inclusions. These might be such things as garden sheds, pool equipment, a dishwasher, expensive light fittings — even some furniture.

So, the rule with inclusions is this: exclude all but the basics at first and then offer other inclusions when negotiating.

# 120 Do I need to declutter?

Yes, you do need to declutter your home. Too many people accumulate too much 'stuff'.

You must get rid of all the clutter. Even more so if clutter has morphed into hoarding.

Consider what will happen to your 'stuff' when you die. How much will go with you? So, get rid of clutter; get a better price and enjoy your life.

A garage sale is also worth considering: 'turn your trash into cash'.

If you have too much trash and you can't get any cash for it, invest in a skip bin.

Oh, and be careful you don't accidentally sell valuable rare books. They may not look it, but some old books are worth thousands of dollars. If in doubt, check them out.

# 121 Should I have my home staged?

It depends. Buyers are wary of phoniness. They seek reality. They love homes filled with love and warmth. If you own such a home, you probably don't need to stage it. But if your home is dated or cluttered or the furniture is stale, staging can be a good investment.

Here is the ultimate answer on the subject of staging: *If staging increases the value of your home by much more than the cost of staging, do it.*

Sometimes, a large mirror or a beautiful painting can make a room feel more spacious and appealing.

Also, be careful with displaying a floor plan of your home before buyers inspect it. Floor plans can make homes appear smaller. You don't want buyers rejecting your home before they inspect it because they mistakenly feel it's too small.

## The benefits of staging

Scott Kim is an agent in Melbourne. He loathes the needless costs that many agents thrust on home sellers. He accepts no money for himself — or via himself — for any reason until homes are sold and sellers are happy. Staging, of course, is an outside cost, rarely tied with the agent (although less reputable agents pocket kickbacks from stylists). Scott needs to be supremely confident that all dollars spent by sellers can be justified.

Scott writes:

Staging adds a genuine sense of 'modernness'. Most homes are a mixture — some parts old and some parts new. A good stylist modernises homes and adds (never detracts) to the home's basic charm and character. The stylist brings the right sized furniture, with matching colour schemes. Styling can make a home flow better. It can create the additional space that many homes need especially those that have extra-large furniture for comfort; but styled homes have ideal sized furniture. This gives the appearance of enlarging bedrooms and living areas.

Styling can increase a home's value. Sometimes massively. Scott believes that for every dollar you spend, you should get at least five dollars in return. Therefore, a spend of, say, $3000, can easily add an extra $15000 to your home's sale price. Often much more.

# 122 How much does it cost to stage and 'spruce up' a home?

Scott Kim says, 'There are seven main areas where we recommend homeowners consider spending money to spruce up their homes and improve their sale price'.

They are:

1.  *Styling/staging*: typically $2500–$5500
2.  *Kitchen renovation*: $25 000–$35 000
3.  *Bathroom renovation*: $20 000–$25 000
4.  *Painting walls/ceilings/external*: $5000–$15 000 depending on the amount of painting needed
5.  *Lighting (for lower 2.4-metre ceiling homes)*: get rid of hanging pendant lights that lower the ceiling height and install flush mounted LED downlights. This adds heaps of light. Downlights only cost about $70 per downlight supplied and fitted. You can completely turn a dark/depressing home into a much brighter and happier space

6. *Flooring (new carpets, polished timber floors or floating floors)*:
floating floors only cost around $80 per square metre supplied
and fitted. If you have a home with a mix of timber floors, tiles
and carpet, all in different areas of the home, it can make a
house seem dated. Some demographics love low maintenance
(no carpets), so we often suggest you put floating floors
throughout. This brings brightness into the house (especially
with modern hybrid light oak-coloured floors). It makes the
home seem spacious and modern

7. *Gardening:* Scott never does anything crazy with gardening.
Just neat, tidy and clean lines between grass and garden bed
with mulch is usually enough.

# 123 Do you have examples of how staging and 'sprucing' increase the final sale price of a home?

Yes, absolutely.

In Scott Kim's agency, he can cite dozens of cases where sellers
invested in staging and increased the value of their homes. The average
cost of styling is about $4000. Sure, that's a lot of money for a lot of
sellers. But Scott has seen returns of 20 times the amount invested on
styling. Importantly, he has never seen a seller invest in styling and
not get a profitable return.

Scott reveals:

> We sold two neighbouring homes in one year. The first
> home we sold fetched $1.2 million. It was arguably a
> nicer home, with a granny flat at the rear. We sold this
> in the month of October. The owners did not accept our
> recommendation to stage their home. Buyers constantly
> described it as 'sad' and 'dated'.

After it sold, the neighbours hired us as their agents. They agreed with our advice to have their home styled. Once it happened, everyone (from owners to buyers) said, 'This home *feels* so good'. It had a happy vibe. We sold this second home — in a slower market in the following October — remember, technically, the first home was better — for $1.29 million. An extra $90 000.

Scott is sure that styling increased the value of the second home by at least $100 000. A great return for an investment of $4500.

Scott says:

We also have several wonderful examples of how sprucing up (usually minor renovating) a home can massively increase the value. One memorable example was a home which we attempted to sell twice. It was in Wilga Street. At our first attempt, the home was in its original condition. It had purple carpets without furniture. The very best offer we could get was $1.1 million. The owners wanted to accept this price — despite our recommendation to the contrary — but then they had a major upheaval in their family. So, they took the home off the market, promising to come back to us later. Sure enough, they returned and asked us to have a second attempt at selling the home. As the market had not risen, they feared they may get less than they were previously offered (as often happens). But then we suggested they renovate the home. We offered to project manage it for them.

After completing the renovation (cost $41 500) we advised the owners to invest a bit more (about $3500) and style the home. Finally, it was ready to be offered for sale — in its freshly spruced and styled condition.

What happened next was amazing (yet not uncommon). The home sold within six days and at a record price for the street. We managed to negotiate several offers (under our silent offer system) with the highest offer at $1.501 million.

An extra $401 000 for a total spruce-up and style investment of $45 000.

My message to all homeowners is this: at least *consider* improving your home. Some agents don't recommend renovating — but often for selfish reasons. They want their commission fast. Sprucing and styling can take up to three months.

We feel it's worth the wait if just for one reason: the delight on the faces of our clients at the increased value of their homes.

# 124 Should I have an open house or allow set appointments?

A golden rule in selling is 'Make it easy for buyers to buy'.

Having a home available to inspect for 30 minutes a week does not make it easy for buyers. Many buyers can't make the allotted time. Contrary to what agents claim, some buyers do not come back. They go to other homes at times to suit them.

The main reason that agents do open inspections is not primarily to sell homes. It's to find more sellers. Many agents string out open inspections (and keep the homes unsold) because they're a good source of leads. One real estate trainer wrote, 'The worst thing you can do is sell the house that's open for inspection'.

Having hundreds of stickybeaks wandering through your home is not good for its value.

Don't open your home to lookers. But make sure it's always available to genuine buyers who have been qualified (see question 162) and identified. The words 'Genuine buyers may inspect any time to suit' will help you sell to the best buyers for the best price.

Be careful. Open homes are a security risk. Most agents just ask for a name and a phone number and don't bother to verify the details. Burglars do not leave their real names. Also, your home is probably not insured during open inspections. Check with your insurance company.

Better still, reject open inspections. Have inspections by appointment only.

Make it clear that any time is the right time for the right buyer to insect your home.

# 125 Must I have my property ready to inspect all the time?

This seems like a negative question. So, let me give you a one-word answer, then explain the reasoning.

Yes.

Here is another question: When are you ready to sell to a buyer who offers you a great price? Surely the answer is 'always'. So surely your home should be available for inspection whenever a qualified buyer wants to inspect it. (The process of qualifying buyers is explained in question 162.)

You don't have to keep your home looking like a show home. Just ensure it is clean. A pair of slippers near the bed, a wet shower, dishes in the kitchen sink, the sound of a washing machine. This is part of daily living.

Buyers understand living conditions. They also appreciate being allowed to inspect a property at a time that suits them.

# 126 How do I know who is coming to look at my home?

If your agent has identified and qualified the buyer, you will know exactly who's inspecting your home. Unfortunately, many agents have no idea who's inspecting your home — especially at open inspections.

For safety reasons, it's common sense to insist that all people who wish to inspect your home be identified and qualified. Two questions need to be answered and known by you: 'Who are they?' and 'Can they afford our home?' If you can't get answers to these questions, don't allow them to see your home. You are not a museum for stickybeaks.

# 127 How long do inspections take and how much notice should I receive beforehand?

Provided that prospective buyers are identified and qualified, you should allow them to spend as much time as they require. In the modern era, most homes cost at least $1 000 000. And yet many buyers get better treatment when they buy fuel for their car than when buying a home for their family.

It defies belief that most agents hold a home open for inspection for 30 minutes a week. If a buyer arrives near the end of the allotted time, the agent will be rushing to the next home.

If you want the best price for your home, find the best agent: one who will give the best buyers as much time as they need. This is how you get the best price.

As for advance notice, most agents are reasonable — so are most buyers. Generally, you will get at least 60 minutes' notice. Ideally, a couple of hours. Perhaps a day or two. However, there may be occasions when you only get a few minutes. Don't worry. As long as your home is clean, it need not be pristine. Lived-in homes look lived-in.

Be willing to welcome the right buyer at a moment's notice.

# 128 Should I stay in my home during inspections?

If possible, you should vacate your home while it's being inspected. Always do what makes buyers feel comfortable. If owners are at home, buyers may feel uneasy. They won't spend as much time in the home, and they will be less inclined to make comments.

If you must be at home when buyers inspect, get out of the way. Go into the garden or to the least attractive part of your home.

Whatever you do, stay away from the most pleasant part of your home.

Allow buyers space to look and roam. Don't rush them.

# 129 What is the most important point when presenting my home?

Smell. If your home stinks, the price will sink.

People are attracted to homes like they are attracted to people. The number one attraction factor is scent.

The aroma in your home will be the first — and most memorable — factor for visitors. But few people have the courage to tell you if your home stinks.

Although bad smells in a home are about the worst turn-off, they are often not apparent to the home's owners. If your house stinks, you get used to it.

So, ask your friends (those with courage) to tell you. It'll be hard to find an agent honest or courageous enough to tell you that your house stinks. For your own sake, encourage feedback. Don't shoot the messenger. Be objective. Face facts no matter how unpleasant.

Consider removing pets from your home, especially during inspections. And never allow pets to approach buyers. Whether smelly, friendly or hostile, pets will not improve your chance of selling. You may like your pets more than humans, but humans buy homes.

Be sure you remove smelly items such as a kitty litter, open garbage and bad fridge food, and address bathroom/lavatory smells. For a few dollars you can buy scented plug-ins from a supermarket. Some candles can also emit a beautiful scent.

Even though it's a bit of a gimmick, a delicious cake baking in the oven is a nice smell.

### On the nose

While I'm writing this book, my new dog—a beautiful red cattle dog called Ruby—is lying at my feet. She is only a puppy but already seems like the best dog I've ever had. Except for one factor. She has the smelliest farts. I've expelled her from my study several times while writing. I've also consumed several cans of air freshener.

# 130 What is the main factor that inspires people to buy a home?

Love. The most powerful force on earth.

No matter how it's sold—auction, tender, private—buyers who love a home will want it.

And they will do all they possibly can to buy it. They will get a bigger loan from their bank; they will borrow (or accept) money from their family; and they will sell their toys. Some may even get a second (or third) job to buy a home they love.

Of course, the best part — from a seller's perspective — of owning a home that a buyer (or many buyers) love is that you get a better price. Especially if your agent is a good negotiator.

I have seen heart buyers (as I call them) pay hundreds of thousands of dollars above what agents call 'market value'. On high-end properties — especially those in short supply (in 'tightly held' areas) — it's not unusual to see heart buyers pay millions of dollars more. Sadly, as happens in most cases, sellers rarely receive the extra dollars from a heart buyer. This is entirely due to the sellers hiring the wrong agents.

When agents are attuned to the real desires of home buyers, home sellers get the best price for their homes.

# 131 How can I make my home more loveable?

You need to be loveable yourself.

Homes, just like people, develop personalities. We can all walk into a home and detect a mood. We feel the aura. As someone once wrote, 'If there is joy in the home there is love in the heart'. Joyous homes are the most attractive of all because they make people fall in love with them. Like joyful people.

But just as loveable homes emit a loving aura, loveless homes exude a terrible aura. If a home is being sold due to marital collapse or if there is aggravation or worse, violence, in the home, there will likely be something about that home that repels buyers. This is why some homes take a long time to sell. Or why they attract extremely low offers.

It's hard to put love into a loveless home — but here are some suggestions that may help:

- If you are in dispute with your partner, it may be best that one of you vacates.
- Consider whether the aura of the home could be improved if it is totally vacant.
- Have a major (bond-style) clean.
- Consider having an honest and professional stylist give you advice.
- Consider staging the home.
- Spruce up the entrance to your home — even if you have to pay a skilled gardener.
- Consider minor renovations, especially areas of the home that are unattractive.
- Make sure the home smells nice.
- Remove anything controversial or likely to offend (like political posters).

And finally, here are three features that can make a home more loveable.

1. *Cleanliness.* Don't mistake cleanliness for tidiness. Some tidy homes are cold. But an untidy home — if it is clean and doesn't stink — can be filled with love. Stop pretending. No-one wants to live in a museum. Being clean is more important than being tidy.
2. *Warmth.* You can add warmth to your home with such items as photographs, quaint cushions, heirlooms, flowers, fresh fruit, natural light, spaciousness and, if you have one — and it's winter — an open fire.

3. *Guys and gals.* The most important room in a home for most women is the kitchen, followed by the bathroom. For men it's the size of the garage followed by the rumpus room. And remember the children. A child-friendly home appeals to children. Even a basketball hoop can be exciting to a child.

# 132 What is a 'love list' — and do I need one?

A love list is a list of all that you love about your home and your area. It should include what first attracted you to your home; what you have grown to love while you've owned it; any improvements you have made — and, most importantly, the happiness it has brought you.

This list should include at least a dozen points. Some people list several dozen. I once saw a list prepared by elderly homeowners that had 127 factors they loved, right down to the benefit of having great neighbours.

This list should be headed 'Love list', followed by the words, 'What we love about our home and our community'. It may be several pages long. Ideally, you should have a photo at the top of the first page showing either the front of your home or the part you love most.

Several copies of this document should be handed to your agent. You can also leave copies in a prominent spot in your home so that potential buyers can take a copy.

A love list is a great ally in helping you achieve a great result.

If/when a buyer makes a lower offer for your home and gives you a list of reasons (complaints) to justify their offer, you can push back with your love list.

# 133 If I sell an investment property, should it be vacant?

In most cases, no.

Many agents advise landlords to vacate investment properties when selling. They say this makes it easier for buyers to inspect the property.

But the reason some agents want the investment property empty is darker. Most landlords have repayments. An empty property means no income. And no income means more pressure on the owners. And more pressure on the owners forces them to lower their price. And the lower the price, the easier the property is to sell ... and the sooner the agent gets paid.

If you have a clean and decent tenant — especially one who's rented long term and who pays promptly and seldom complains — why not be considerate?

Here's how to create a proverbial win-win situation. Instead of you having no income and your tenant having nowhere to live, lower the rent while the property is for sale. This can be done in return for the tenant's cooperation in keeping the property clean and allowing inspections at different times. Make sure the discount is given once the property is sold. Not at the beginning. This inspires the tenants to keep their word.

So, if it takes you 10 weeks to sell the property and you give the tenant a discount on their rent of $200 per week, you will credit them $2000 once the property is sold. Should the property sell to an occupier, you will give your tenant ample time to find another home.

An occupied property that is well kept will always be appealing to buyers.

And here's an incredible point that some agents never tell you. In many areas — especially when a market is booming — thousands of investors from other states and countries buy properties without inspecting them. So maybe your tenants will barely notice the change in ownership.

Keep your tenant, keep your income, increase your chance of a better price.

## Key takeaways from part 7

▶ Don't be too hasty to give away too many inclusions.

▶ Declutter your home. If it's a mess it will sell for less.

▶ Staging a home might increase your final sale price. It's worth doing the maths.

▶ Know the seven main areas in your home where you can increase its value.

▶ Allow genuine buyers to inspect your home any time that suits them.

▶ Your home may not be insured if you hold an open house.

▶ Hordes of 'lookers' benefit agents, but not you as a home seller.

▶ Only allow identified and qualified potential buyers to inspect your home.

▶ The most important point in attracting people to your home is its smell.

▶ The best-paying buyers are those who fall in love with your home.

▶ Prepare and circulate a love list.

▶ If possible, keep a good tenant when selling an investment property.

▶ The best presented homes attract the best buyers and sell for the best prices.

# <u>PART 8</u>

# MARKETING YOUR HOME

In this part, you will discover how you can reduce or eliminate marketing costs and get a higher price for your home.

The main reason agents are eager for you to spend your hard-earned dollars on marketing is to promote themselves and to find new leads. Real estate marketing is riddled with misinformation.

There are 195 countries in the world. Australia is the only country where most agents persuade sellers to pay for marketing costs *plus* hefty commission. And increasingly, many agents in New Zealand are emulating Australian agents, asking sellers to pay additional advertising costs (even though their commission is often twice as high!).

In all other countries, marketing costs are included in the commission. So it's important to learn how to stand up to agents who expect you to fork out thousands in marketing costs even if your home is not sold (or if it sells below the price quoted when you signed up). It's your home. You are the boss. You hire the agent. You set the terms. If the agent does not like your terms, find a better agent.

It might surprise you to learn that the best homes are often not advertised, and yet they often sell for higher prices than homes that are.

Among the questions and answers that follow, you'll discover the 12 biggest truths about real estate marketing. By the end of this part, you will know how to save thousands of dollars — and how to protect your home's value from being damaged by excessive and needless advertising

## Questions in this part

134.  What do I need to know about advertising?
135.  What is a digital footprint and should I worry about it?
136.  What is the best source of advertising?
137.  Why do agents want me to pay advertising costs in advance?
138.  Are pay-later advertising schemes worth considering?
139.  It's my home; surely, it's fair that I pay for the advertising?
140.  What is the worst source of advertising?
141.  What does 'activity conditioning' mean?
142.  How should a home be promoted or advertised?
143.  What are effective ways to advertise real estate without paying outrageous costs?
144.  Do I need professional photography?
145.  Do I need a video or drone shots of my property?
146.  Should I advertise on several websites?
147.  Is it essential to advertise on realestate.com.au?
148.  Who writes the advertisement for my property?
149.  How do I write an advertisement that's most likely to get the best result?
150.  Is it necessary to pay thousands of dollars for a premium or upgraded ad?
151.  If agents offer 'upgraded' ads to all sellers, how can they possibly all get a special deal?
152.  Doesn't more advertising and more open homes mean I'll get more prospective buyers?

# 134 What do I need to know about advertising?

The most important fact to know about real estate advertising is the pernicious practice of VPA.

VPA, which stands for vendor paid advertising, is a scheme where agents persuade home sellers to pay the (usually inflated) cost of advertising their homes in addition to the commission. Incredibly, most agents expect sellers to pay these advertising costs — which often amount to thousands of dollars — in advance of their home being sold or if they withdraw from sale. If a home is not sold (as often happens), the sellers suffer a large loss, but the agent and website operators profit greatly.

VPA is the major reason why Australia has become one of the most expensive places in the world to sell a home. As all agents are aware, however, the main purpose of VPA is to promote agents, not properties. The other major purpose of VPA is to find leads for agents — again, at the expense of sellers.

While most agents push the VPA scheme in Australia, sellers can and should reject it.

> *Simply tell the agent that you will not pay anything until your home is sold. That's a golden rule of selling a home.*

Here are the 12 biggest truths about real estate advertising.

1. *Real estate advertising in Australia is a multi-billion-dollar industry.* There is approximately 50 times more advertising today than in pre-internet times and yet there are not even double the number of homes sold. Most real estate advertising is unnecessary — at least when it comes to *causing* sales.

The focus of the major property websites is profit, not serving the community. While this might be understandable, don't let them profit through making you think that advertising is essential to sell your home. It's not. Many homes sell for better prices when not advertised.

2. *If 95 per cent of real estate advertising disappeared, the number of sales made would not change.* Buyers don't buy homes because homes are advertised. They buy homes because they like the homes.

3. *In Australia, around a million people a week view real estate ads online, yet only around 10 000 people buy a home.* So, at least 990 000 people who view real estate ads each week are not buyers that week. They are viewers. Don't spend thousands of dollars advertising your home to viewers. You want buyers. In fact, all you want is one buyer — the one who pays you the best price.

4. *A major purpose of real estate advertising is not to promote homes, it's to promote agents.* A favourite word in the real estate industry is 'profile'. Agents are obsessed with what's called 'building a profile'. Suburbs are filled with advertisements for real estate agents. Agents love increasing their profile at the expense of sellers. Many laugh about it. The industry gives awards to agents who persuade sellers to spend the most money on advertising.

    If agents want to plaster their faces over billboards and bus stops, let them pay for it. Not you. A golden rule for home sellers is *never pay any money before your home is sold*.

5. *Many agents refuse to list homes today unless sellers pay thousands of dollars (or agree to pay later) for advertising.* These agents are not only arrogant and lazy, they're also stupid. Reject them immediately.

6. *Many buyers skip past prominently advertised homes.* They think these homes will be too expensive (overpriced) or there must be something wrong for them to be so widely promoted. As advertising executives know, a small ad is usually more effective than a big ad. Oh sure, it's not as effective at attracting lookers and stickybeaks, nor at bringing in more leads for agents. But inexpensive ads attract buyers. Buyers are resourceful. They find homes for sale. They chase agents, even lazy ones. They spend hours online. They drive around an area. Sometimes a sign on a home is all that's needed to get the best price for that home.

7. *All agents have buyers waiting to buy homes.* Many of today's agents don't bother calling interested buyers on their books about a new listing. Instead, they tell buyers to follow their advertisements and call them if they see a home they like. A well-known saying about advertising is, 'Advertising is what salespeople do when they're too lazy to follow up prospects'. Tell your agent to get to work instead of wasting your money on needless advertising.

8. *You go to an agent because, as a seller, you literally want to buy a buyer.* Just like you go to a butcher to buy meat. Butchers don't ask for money to find cows. So, agents shouldn't ask for money to find buyers. All businesses need to promote themselves. But most real estate agents expect clients to pay to promote their business. Don't fall for it.

9. *A marketing campaign for one home can often mean three or four extra sales for the agent.* Agents will tell sellers, 'It's your house — you should pay the cost of advertising it'. Decent sellers think this is fair. They don't realise that agents use the ads to attract new leads for themselves. The naïve sellers who fund these campaigns don't get the benefits (or a share in the commission) from the sales that come from that campaign.

> *Don't be gaslighted into forking out money for real estate advertising.*

10. *Advertising can seriously damage the value of your home.* If you advertise and don't sell in a couple of weeks, the world knows that your home is being shunned. This plays into agents' hands. Advertising then helps agents condition you down in price. Protect the value of your home by either not advertising or doing minimal advertising. (See point 12 below.)

11. *Most agents have slick lines to persuade sellers to spend money on advertising.* Such as: 'You can't sell a secret'. Such a statement proves their lack of negotiation knowledge. Secrets *do* sell — and often for more than homes that are promoted — because secrets appear special. Many buyers value privacy and safety. Only advertise your home as a last resort.

12. *The more you advertise a home, the less you'll get for it.* If you must advertise, go small. Don't fall into the trap set by websites and agents who say, 'The more you spend on advertising, the more you'll get for your home'. The reverse is more correct.

If it *were* true that more advertising meant a bigger sale price, why not advertise on television? Why not spend tens, even hundreds, of thousands of dollars? Why advertise only in Australia? What about overseas? There's no limit to wastage with advertising. Those who profit from it claim that advertising is 'an investment'. Sure, the more you 'invest', the more they profit.

The most important point about real estate advertising is this: Most is a waste of money. Don't let it be your family's money that gets wasted.

# 135 What is a digital footprint and should I worry about it?

A digital footprint is the path left online about a property.

It is important to understand the concept of digital footprints. How they can hurt you and how they can help you. If you are buying, they can give you plenty of information about a property—although much of it is inaccurate and needs to be treated with caution. If you are selling, digital footprints cause trouble. For most homeowners, it means the interior of their home is available for anybody to see. And yes, that means anybody—good, bad or indifferent. Burglars follow digital footprints. And so do stalkers and killers. (See question 15.)

The digital age is absurdly, recklessly and needlessly dangerous.

Agents, buyers, neighbours, stickybeaks, the media and all your friends and family can likely discover all about your property with a few keystrokes. They will know what you paid for a home, when you bought it, when you decided to sell it, how long you have had it for sale, the price you want for it and, worst of all, there will be a computer-generated estimate of your home's value. Much of this information will be wrong. It can be damaging when you are selling. And misleading when you are buying.

So yes, you should worry about digital footprints.

# 136 What is the best source of advertising?

To answer this question accurately we need to define what is meant by 'best' and what is meant by 'source'. In real estate, there is a big difference between perception and reality.

One of the biggest mistakes made with real estate marketing is that agents — urged on by the major websites — focus on *quantity* of enquiries instead of *quality* of enquiries. The bigger the quantity, the bigger the cost to home sellers. And the bigger the benefit to the agents and the advertising websites.

But given that you can only sell your home to one buyer, you need to reach that buyer in the most economical manner. Most real estate advertising is not feasible. It's not designed that way. The advertisers don't place the interests of sellers ahead of their own interests. They devote themselves to figuring out how they can charge the most and justify their huge cost to home sellers (via agents who are their army of pushy salespeople). The big 'sell' commonly works like this: 'When you advertise with us you reach millions of buyers'. To the uninitiated it sounds good. But sellers who consider most real estate advertising soon realise that what's made to appear the best way to sell is, in reality, the worst — especially on a cost-effective basis.

Searching for the best buyer for your home can be compared to searching for the proverbial needle in a haystack. Why pay for straw?

But if you blow away the unwanted hay, the needle becomes visible. You find it faster and you find it cheaper. That's the essence of smart economical marketing. That's what should be called 'the best source of advertising'.

The advertising that finds the right buyer in the most cost-effective manner is the best source of advertising.

Major real estate websites boast that they get 1 million visitors a day, which of course is 7 million visitors per week. But given that there are around 10 000 homes sold every week in Australia, which is spread across 2644 post codes, this means that 6 990 000 of the people you are being charged to reach are not buyers. They are lookers. And, of the remaining 10 000 genuine buyers, there may be as few as one or two buying in your area.

So clearly, it's financial stupidity to pay to reach seven million people when, at best, only a handful want to buy in your area.

You don't want a large number of lookers; you want a small number of qualified buyers.

It's nuts to pay upwards of $5000 to reach millions of people who won't buy your home.

## A revolution is underway

The cost of advertising on major websites is absurdly expensive. The greed of these websites seems insatiable, the more so since they created the impression that they are indispensable. They are constantly raising their prices and figuring out more ways to convince home sellers to spend more money.

Thankfully, after years of complaints, in 2025, the federal authority—the ACCC (the Australian Competition and Consumer Commission)—launched an ongoing enquiry into the business methods of Australia's largest real estate website.

History teaches us, however, that there are dire consequences of insatiable greed. Whether it be Louis XVI and the French Revolution in the late 1700s or the modern real estate industry, there comes a time when exploited people say 'enough'. They rise up and create their own revolution.

This is starting to happen in real estate today. Community websites are springing up daily. Their purpose is to help people sell or buy real estate at low or no advertising cost.

And yes, they are attracting thousands of members each. And to their delight, agents, sellers and buyers are discovering that it's possible to find the right buyers without the exorbitant

> costs charged by websites owned by billionaires. The word is spreading.
>
> A new source of advertising is arriving. And it's bringing with it less cost and the same or better selling price for the homeowners.

# 137 Why do agents want me to pay advertising costs in advance?

The reason agents demand money in advance is because their service is so poor, they know the sellers won't pay later.

Some real estate firms should be known as 'Grabit and Run Real Estate'.

As I've said before, *don't pay any money—especially for advertising—before your home is sold.*

# 138 Are pay-later advertising schemes worth considering?

No. Never. As more sellers have become resistant to paying advertising costs, a number of pay-later schemes have emerged. These are grubby high-interest moneylenders. If you read the fine print in their contracts, you would never touch them.

Whether you are asked to pay money in advance for advertising or you are offered a pay-later scheme, you should refuse. I can't repeat this point too often: *pay only upon success.*

# 139 It's my home; surely, it's fair that I pay for the advertising?

No. Not at all. Anyone who asks a question like this is clearly decent but naïve to the workings of the real estate industry. Agents use the statement, 'It's your home, you should pay the costs' to guilt sellers into paying.

> *The main purpose of advertising is to promote agents.*

Advertising attracts other sellers for the agency. This gives the agents more commission. If you pay the cost of advertising, you should be entitled to any commission that comes from that advertising.

Don't fall for the 'it's your home' argument. It's spurious.

# 140 What is the worst source of advertising?

The worst source of advertising is one that costs far too much in dollars and has far too many disadvantages. Like major real estate websites.

A major real estate website should be your last choice, not your first choice. Before you risk thousands of dollars to reach millions of non-buyers, you should attempt to sell your home without needless costs and without damaging its value. Indeed, as you are about to see, avoiding major websites can lead to a far superior selling price.

Listed below are some important reasons why advertising on major real estate websites can be the worst source of advertising.

- *It risks turning your home into a lemon.* Major website advertising can quickly turn your home into a lemon. When a property is known as a 'lemon' it means that it has *appeared* to have failed to sell.

  The most common examples are 'auction lemons'. If you are persuaded to sell by auction, you will also be persuaded to spend (waste) thousands of dollars advertising on a major website. It can't be overstressed: most homes offered for sale by auction don't sell at the auction.

  Genuine buyers — especially bargain hunters — watch real estate ads like hawks. As soon as they see homes not sold at auction, they know they are seeing auction lemons.

- *Mass advertising can force your price down.* Many homes in certain suburbs are similar, at least in outward appearance. This is particularly so in newer areas, where homes have often been mass-built by the same builders. Sure, some homes may have been renovated, and others may have extra benefits. But the moment you allow your home to be advertised on a major website, your home is forced to compete with comparable homes in the same area. The major way that lookalike homes compete with each other is on price. The owners who are willing to accept the lowest price are those whose homes are usually sold first.

  This is known as 'comparative marketing'. It's one of the worst ways to achieve a good price. It means that price rules. The price of your home is tethered to similar homes. For example, if the owner of a similar property to yours is in financial trouble and decides to slash their price, your price gets dragged down too.

And this, of course, forces down the prices of other homes because agents and buyers compare your home to a similar home that sold cheaply. The fact that other owners may have been under financial pressure is irrelevant. Their cheap price means buyers will expect you to sell for a cheap price. If you dig in and refuse to drop your price, your home can become a lemon. And offers will then get even lower.

If you own a property that is similar to many other properties in the same area, the worst way to advertise — if you want a good price — is by tossing your property into the comparison market.

### Expensive advertising vs hard work

An investor owned an apartment in an outer-Melbourne suburb. It was similar to hundreds of apartments. Unfortunately, like thousands of investors across Australia, this owner had purchased the property from a wealth-creation company. Their main ploy was to sell overpriced properties.

Even though this investor had owned the property for almost 10 years, its market value had not reached the price he paid for it. The sums were simple. The property owed him $305 000 but similar properties were selling for around $260 000.

When a local agent was told that the seller needed to sell for $305 000, the agent's instant response was, 'We'll never get that price because as soon as we advertise on the internet everyone will see it's overpriced'.

The owner said, 'Well, we shouldn't advertise it then'.

The agent gave a reply common to incompetent agents: 'How are we going to sell it if we can't advertise it?'

Hard work, that's how.

> Ironically, even though the apartment was similar in outward appearance to others, it had many advantages over most apartments in the area. It was well located in a well-kept building. It had been leased to a reliable tenant who had kept it in excellent condition for 10 years.
>
> The owner was recommended to a young agent from outside the area. Instead of advertising, this super-keen agent began calling investors known to the agency.
>
> The agent soon lined up three inspections. Within a week, he had a firm offer of $312000.

The best homes are often not advertised.

Superior agents often refuse to advertise homes on major websites. Instead, they call their contacts. They use the hard-work method, which produces excellent results.

If more agents had more intelligence and more integrity, coupled with excellent negotiation skills, more owners would receive far better prices for their properties.

Many of the best homes are never advertised. It's often inferior homes that need to be advertised. It's been that way for centuries. It's an economic fact. High advertising might lead to a sale — but at a lower price than if owners hired a smart, hard-working agent.

# 141 What does 'activity conditioning' mean?

An essential part of conditioning is creating lots of activity to prove to sellers that their price is too high.

The main types of activity used by agents include advertising, open inspections, fake offers, negative feedback and bad economic news. Anything some agents can do to remove the blame away from the agent and place it somewhere else.

Sellers must be careful not to demand too much visible action from agents because they will get action that works against them.

The best agents do not indulge in activity conditioning. The best agents are working constantly behind the scenes to find the best buyers. They are not standing at open inspections waving hundreds of lookers through a home and then calling the owners with negative feedback.

The best agents have one goal: to find the best buyer who will pay the best price. Without activity conditioning.

# 142 How should a home be promoted or advertised?

Agents think that marketing means advertising. But smart marketers know that marketing needs to be cost-effective and attractive.

Most home sellers get duped into spending too much money in the wrong areas. Why spend thousands of dollars to reach the same buyers that you could reach for a fraction of the cost — even at zero cost? Efficiency and effectiveness — that's what smart marketing is about.

Most agents use what's known as a scatter-gun approach. They advertise to anyone and everyone. But you need a competent agent who understands that a laser gun approach — which means focusing on finding the right buyer — is a more efficient and effective method. There is no benefit whatsoever to sellers if masses of unqualified stickybeaks see or inspect their home.

The best place to advertise a home is where there is the best chance of finding the best buyer for that home. By far the best source of advertising is word of mouth — especially for properties that have not been widely commercially promoted. If you must advertise, choose a medium that will reach the same buyers for a lower cost than commonly used methods.

As with so much that happens in real estate, think before you act. Think before you waste thousands of dollars on needless advertising.

# 143 What are effective ways to advertise real estate without paying outrageous costs?

There are many ways of finding buyers for a home without paying thousands of dollars to major website companies. But many agents do deals with website companies. The agents guarantee the website companies that *all* the agents' sellers will be forced to pay several thousand dollars in advertising costs. This is regardless of whether such costs are necessary.

You can get a better price for your home without paying media-owned mega-websites. At least give it a try. The worst that can happen is that you are no worse off. The best that can happen is that you save thousands of dollars.

Here are seven ways to effectively market your home — either by yourself or with an agent.

1. *Tell the neighbours.* Many homes are purchased by buyers who live close to the home. In some cases the sellers have forked out thousands of dollars for needless advertising. A classic example was a family farm that sold for close to $30 million to

a neighbour. But the agent had persuaded the owners to spend almost $100 000 in advertising costs. Please don't assume that $30 million is such a lot of money that it doesn't matter if you waste $100 000. Look at each amount in isolation: $100 000 is a lot of money. It can be put to better use than being given to a major media company.

And in case you're wondering why this agent (as happens with most agents) didn't approach the neighbours prior to asking the sellers to spend thousands of dollars in advertising, the reason is simple: many agents are lazy. They also like to use the marketing expenses to promote themselves. It might be unethical, but it is common.

2. *Tell your circle.* One of the simplest, easiest and fastest ways to find a great buyer for your home is to put the word out among your 'circle'. This includes your family, your friends, your work colleagues and anyone with whom you have regular contact. Just tell them that you're thinking of selling your home — and watch what happens. Chances are you'll get several calls from people keen to inspect your home.

   Your agent can approach your circle if you don't wish to do it yourself. But imagine having to pay an agent $50 000 in commission if your best friend buys your house. Hence why it's important to have a Sole Agency Agreement instead of an Exclusive Agency Agreement. (For more information on agreements, see question 46, point 8.)

3. *Hand out leaflets locally.* Have a few hundred leaflets printed about your home. These leaflets can be distributed to all the homes within a few hundred metres of yours. The best agents will door-knock hundreds of local homeowners and hand out leaflets for a newly listed home. These agents will let locals know that they are the first to be offered this home. This

creates both the scarcity and urgency effect in negotiation and selling.

One agent uses a headline on a leaflet that reads, 'This home could win a heart'. He has an image of a heart above the photograph of the property. This agent knows that many (if not most) heart buyers (those who fall in love with a home) come from the local area. Heart buyers will always pay a better price than ordinary buyers. It's the power of love.

Leaflets to homeowners in your local area are a magnificent marketing opportunity.

4. *Advertise in the local newspaper.* Although local newspapers are dying out, there are still areas where papers exist. They are eagerly read by locals. A small, classified advertisement (for less than $100) or even a display advertisement (costing around $200) could yield an excellent result.

   In place of (or as well as) newspapers, some areas — especially regional centres — have volunteers who print monthly news bulletins. They gratefully accept advertising at near negligible costs. They will be delighted to hear from you. And you may be delighted in the result.

5. *Advertise on social media.* Social media is the modern way to reach the masses. It can often be done economically — especially if you target your individual market. Community Facebook pages often allow you to promote your property.

   There are also hundreds of Facebook groups where you can advertise your home at minimal or no charge. These groups have thousands of members, all of whom are interested in selling or buying property, often in a specific region.

There is likely a Facebook group available to suit every type of property in Australia. Savvy agents are getting great results from social media. But they are not encouraged by the powers-that-be (such as networks or franchise bosses or even individual bosses) to use this form of advertising. In at least one case an agent announced to his network — one of the biggest in Australia — that he was getting better results from Facebook than major real estate websites. And, of course, at a fraction of the price. He was then forbidden by his franchise to advertise homes on Facebook. He was astounded. It turns out that a director of the franchise group was a major shareholder in a major website.

6. *Contact property people*. Real estate agents are not the only people involved in real estate. The property industry has many people working in the fringe of the industry. People such as lawyers, conveyancers, valuers, building inspectors, staging companies — even rubbish removal companies. Tell your agent to get in touch with all these people. Like so many sellers, you may sell your home without having to fork out thousands of dollars in advertising costs.

7. *Hit the radio stations*. Here's a surprise. Whether it's commercial radio or community radio, you can now advertise on radio stations for a fraction of the cost of major real estate websites. It's astounding that more people haven't thought of this source. In some cities, radio advertisements can cost as little as $35 for 30 seconds. And you can reach thousands of people. Ads on community radio stations can cost as little as $10 each, and also reach thousands of people.

Always consider different options for marketing your home — assuming that agents don't already have a buyer — instead of instantly agreeing to pay thousands of dollars, which is too costly and not necessary.

# 144 Do I need professional photography?

The *best* thing about professional photography is that it makes you feel good.

The *worst* thing about professional photography is that it annoys buyers. And that makes them hostile. Hostility is not an ingredient that augers well for the best price.

Here's the problem: professional photographers, especially the best ones, are great at making a home look better than its best. Buyers get excited. But later, they're sorely disappointed with the reality. They feel deceived. Some just walk away.

It's okay for photographs to show your home at its best. It's not okay to raise false hope. Adequate photos can often be achieved with a smartphone. Or maybe one of your mates who dabbles in photography. You rarely need to spend thousands of dollars on professional photography.

Photographs of your home should be good enough to attract enquiry from buyers, but not so good as to deceive and upset the buyers. Don't blame the photographer if the photos are too good. Indeed, the best photographers do their job too well — that's the problem.

Photography is a form of advertising. And again, the purpose of advertising is to attract buyers — not to sell homes

# 145 Do I need a video or drone shots of my property?

What would you prefer: that buyers inspect your home in person or online?

The big problem with videos is that buyers think they've inspected your home. But there is nothing better than literally *seeing* a home.

Videos struggle to convey atmosphere. If your home is beautiful and is likely to appeal to buyers, let your home do the selling, not a video. Most times a video is an unnecessary expense. It can work against you. Buyers may have seen your home, but they haven't felt it.

Videos often turn buyers away.

As for drone shots, you should only have them if it will reveal some benefit or feature of your home that is not otherwise visible … and if the drone shots will attract buyers who would not otherwise have been attracted.

In most cases, drone shots are a waste of money. They can make properties look worse, especially homes on smaller allotments where neighbours are close. Drones are likely to magnify minor faults that buyers never knew existed.

The drone phenomenon is mostly a fad. It's another method of extracting more money from sellers.

You should never spend any dollars unless you will get far more return than you spend.

I am not aware of any evidence where drone photography can be traced to an increase in the sale price of any home.

# 146 Should I advertise on several websites?

No. Genuine buyers are diligent and determined. They visit many websites. When they see the same homes on many different websites, they often wonder what's wrong with those homes.

> *Homes that are overadvertised tend to be undersold.*

Don't be drawn in by the slick marketing words and the gaslighting comments of major websites. For example, some may claim that if you don't advertise on their site, you won't sell your home. It's nonsense. Indeed, if you do advertise your home on a major website, you may well sell your home, but at a lower price than if you had protected its value.

It can't be overstated: don't pay to reach millions of lookers. You only need to reach the right buyer. If you must advertise on a real estate website, advertise on one site. The buyer you need will find your home. Count on it.

# 147 Is it essential to advertise on realestate.com.au?

Definitely not.

If selling is the ability to talk someone into doing something regardless of whether they need it or not, then realestate.com.au is the greatest sales outfit in real estate today.

In a few short years, they've managed to convince most agents and sellers that homes can't sell unless they're listed on realestate.com.au.

Many sellers and agents are now finding alternatives to the needless costs and irrelevant lookers on realestate.com.au.

Many of the best homes are not mass advertised.

Protect your home's value and protect your costs by researching more options than a method that erroneously claims to be essential to selling.

# 148 Who writes the advertisement for my property?

The person who writes the description of your property should be whoever can write in the most honest and appealing manner. The purpose of a description is to tell the truth and make a property attractive to those inclined to buy it.

These days many agents are so bad at writing that the best they can do is a list of bullet points with banal clichés. Some agents expect you to pay hundreds of dollars for a copywriter who has not seen your property. If anything, a copywriter may exaggerate the benefits of a property. This will cause more resentment when buyers see the reality.

The big point to remember with advertising words is that they must be good enough to attract the right buyers and then, once the home is inspected, the buyers should be pleased.

It's better to underrate than overrate a description of a home. There's no point attracting people to a home unless they may be interested in buying the home.

It's also becoming increasingly more common for agents to use AI to write property descriptions. Many of these agents fail to check the AI-written description for errors or falsehoods. This frustrates buyers.

# 149 How do I write an advertisement that's most likely to get the best result?

Real estate agents (and by default many homeowners) make terrible mistakes when advertising properties. One of the worst is offering too much information. Always remember that the *purpose* of an advertisement is not to *sell* the property — it's to create an enquiry for the property.

Most homes have some aspect of love and human warmth about them. That's what you should focus on. Here's an example.

## Aiming for the heart

In 2020, a beautiful home in the Sydney suburb of Seaforth was for sale. It was proving hard to sell. The advertisement for the home read like something out of a textbook. It was boring.

So, the owners engaged a real estate advertising writer/supporter. Another advertisement was written: one aimed at heart buyers. When the agent saw the new advertisement, he said it was 'absolutely terrible'. He told the owners that if they used this new advertisement, they had better find a new agent. His professional image was too important to him.

The owners did exactly that. They found another agent who loved the emotionally charged advertisement. She was excited by it. Within days, dozens of prospective buyers were attracted. The home sold for a higher price than the first agent had obtained after months of boring ('professional') advertising.

If you'd like to see the boring ad *and* the 'terrible' emotional ad, please email support@jenman.com.au (attention of Alec Jenman).

# 150 Is it necessary to pay thousands of dollars for a premium or upgraded ad?

*No.*

It is *not* necessary to pay thousands of dollars for an upgraded advertisement. Nonetheless, convincing sellers to waste thousands of dollars on premium or upgraded advertising is rampant in real estate today.

Yes, as previously acknowledged, you may get more lookers with an upgraded ad.

And yes, the agents and the website companies can provide stats and spurious evidence to support their assertion that you must spend thousands of dollars to market your property. But it's mostly nonsense.

The people you want to see your home are genuine and qualified homebuyers (see question 162). Genuine buyers don't look at the first page on a website and stop; they enter their preferences. They find homes for sale, no matter how much the owners pay to promote their homes.

If you are paying thousands of dollars for advertising, you are almost certainly being ripped off. You are definitely paying far more than you need to pay.

### Say no to upgrading

As an executive from a major website who was selling his own house told me, 'The agent asked me to pay $6000 for a premium ad. I told him to get lost. I told him I work for a major real estate website company, and a $100 ad is just as effective as a $6000 ad. Sometimes more so'.

# 151 If agents offer 'upgraded' ads to all sellers, how can they possibly *all* get a special deal?

Ah, now you're beginning to catch on. Well done.

Here's how the pitch goes: each seller is told that they need to get their home viewed ahead of other homes. So, if they pay thousands of dollars extra, their home goes to the top of the list when buyers search online. Sounds good.

But wait. Remember that every homeowner gets the same pitch.

In many agencies, the real estate salespeople are forced to sell upgraded ads to every seller.

So, you might ask, 'How can every home possibly be the first one to come up?'

It's simple. They rotate the ads.

Rotate? Yes, as in 'take turns'.

If 100 people in your area pay to be the first home on a website, each one gets a few minutes before getting dropped down. And then the next one gets a few minutes. And so on.

This is like paying thousands of dollars to Qantas for a first-class seat to London. Fifteen minutes after take-off, the flight attendant tells you to move to economy. You've had your turn. Now get down the back.

# 152 Doesn't more advertising and more open homes mean I'll get more prospective buyers?

The more people who look at your home — regardless of who they are — the more the agents can refer to such lookers as 'the market'.

If your home doesn't sell, the agent will say, 'This is what the market is telling you'.

But lookers are not buyers. So, who are all these people who, every weekend, in that narrow period of 15 to 30 minutes, traipse through your home?

Most people who visit agents' open inspections are not buyers. Surveys indicate that less than 5 per cent plan to buy in the next five years.

So, who on earth are they? Rent-a-crowd? Surely no agent could be so deceptive. Well, believe it. Agents may not pay people to inspect your home. But they encourage anyone capable of walking and breathing to turn up at the open times.

The more people who turn up, the easier it is for agents to condition sellers down in price.

## Key takeaways from part 8

▶ The main purpose of advertising should be to attract enquiries, not to sell your home.

▶ You should never pay (or agree to pay) money in advance for marketing costs.

▶ Any marketing needs to be both cost-effective and attractive.

▶ Agents get many commercial benefits from advertising homes.

▶ Beware agents who use advertising as a conditioning strategy, trying to get you to lower your price.

▶ Believe it—the best buyers are resourceful. They will find your home without you needing to waste thousands of dollars on marketing costs.

*(continued)*

- Don't use a scatter-gun approach when marketing. Use a laser approach to focus on finding the right buyer.
- Be aware of the disadvantages of a digital footprint.
- Advertising on major websites is absurdly expensive—and often unnecessary.
- Contrary to mythology, it is *not* essential to advertise on realestate.com.au.
- If you advertise on many websites, your home will be over-exposed. Too much exposure is like sunburn: it can burn your sale price.
- Glamour photography can mislead and upset buyers.
- Videos allow buyers to make decisions without an inspection. This is not a good thing!
- Advertising is what salespeople do when they are too lazy to follow up leads.
- Make sure a human (who has seen your home) writes any marketing material.
- You do *not* need to pay thousands of dollars for an upgraded/premium advertisement.
- Lookers are not buyers. You only need one buyer—the right one—and the right buyer will often pay a higher price for privacy and a home that's not mass advertised.
- Remember the 12 biggest truths to drastically reduce your costs and increase your final selling price (see question 134).

# PART 9

# NEGOTIATING THE BEST PRICE

In this part, you will discover how a great negotiator can easily sell your home for a much better price than a typical agent. Incredibly, most agents are dreadful negotiators. This is why most homes are undersold. The true value of your home is the highest price at which it can be sold in the present market.

Learn how to recognise those few agents who are truly skilled negotiators.

But be careful: conveying offers back and forth between buyers and sellers does not make an agent a good negotiator. Such agents are just messengers hoping that sellers will say yes to an offer. Which is how most homes are sold.

Always remember that unless your home sells for the highest price that buyers are willing to pay, then your home has been undersold.

The best agents know how to negotiate the best price. The best agents avoid methods that undersell homes, such as auctions (refer to question 96 for more on this). The best agents insist on using a buyers' price declaration (which you can read about in questions 173 and 174).

So, if an agent wants to know the lowest price you are willing to accept, always reply by saying, 'We just wish to sell for the highest price that is available in the current market'. The best agents will know exactly what you mean.

# Questions in this part

175.  Is it true that increasing the price can be successful?

176.  Is it better to sell a home vacant rather than occupied?

177.  How should I respond to the pressure of a deadline offer?

# 153 What do I need to know about the negotiation process?

The most important negotiation tactic is *how to know when buyers are offering their maximum price.*

It's astonishing, but many agents don't know how to do this.

Some agents even say, 'The best way to get buyers to pay their best price is to have an auction and let them fight it out'. Such a comment reveals the agent's lack of negotiation knowledge.

Yes, the price does go up at auction, whereas the price in private negotiation (starting with a displayed price) usually goes down. Therefore, on the surface, it's easy to be fooled into believing that a public auction is the best way to sell. But here is an obvious and overlooked fact: *The reason prices go up at auctions is because they start low.*

The most important price in any sale is the final price. A skilled negotiator knows when buyers are offering their highest price.

There are so many cautionary points in real estate negotiation. It is worth discovering some of them. The difference between knowledge and ignorance in negotiation can amount to hundreds of thousands of dollars on your final sale price.

Here is a common example of sellers not realising that their home has been short-sold.

## Missing out on the buyer's highest price

Let's say the sellers are hoping to sell their home for a million dollars. The agent is doubtful. Maybe the agent tells the sellers, 'You're being a bit optimistic'. But still, the agent agrees to try and get buyers to offer around or above a million dollars.

The seller's instructions seem reasonable: 'Just get us the best price you can'.

A buyer falls in love with the home. The agent does what many agents do: tells the buyers how much the seller will likely accept. One million dollars.

The agent can barely wait to give the sellers the good news. Their home has been sold for the amount they wanted. The sellers are delighted.

The buyers are also delighted. The house is perfect for them—it has everything they hoped to find in a home. But if pressed—if they had encountered a skilled negotiator—they would gladly have paid more for this home.

How much more?

Another half a million dollars.

This scenario—or similar—plays out in thousands of home sales every week. Yes, thousands of sellers miss out on hundreds of thousands of dollars—sometimes millions of dollars.

Why? Because the agent made the error that many agents make. The agent focused on the amount the sellers would accept. Smart negotiators focus on the amount the buyers will pay.

Just because sellers are happy with a price it doesn't mean the price was the buyers' highest price.

Forget focusing on the lowest the sellers will accept. Instead focus on finding the answer to one question: *What is the most these buyers will pay for this house?*

The agent who can answer this question is the agent you should hire.

# 154 Is it best to sell to a cash buyer?

Be careful.

Some buyers (and agents) try to get a lower price by telling sellers, 'This is a cash sale'.

Sounds impressive.

But all property sales are 'cash on completion'. Whatever its source — savings or a loan — it's all cash.

# 155 Are early offers the best offers?

Early offers are often the best. Especially for the best homes.

So often, sellers feel that if they wait, the offers will increase. They will say, 'But we have only just listed for sale'.

Well, how long do you want to wait?

What's more important to you: your sale price or your time on the market? If price is your priority and you get one or more early offers that meet or exceed your (realistic) price estimate, accept the best offer. Provided, of course, that the offered price enables you to achieve your goals. And the buyers have offered you their BHP, which means the buyers' highest price.

Too many sellers reject early offers. And then, weeks — sometimes months — later, they regret their hasty refusal. They are forced to sell for much less.

# 156 Which buyers pay the best price?

Skilled agents know that there are four 'types' of buyers for a home.

1. *Heart buyers.* If buyers fall in love with a home — and usually it's only pre-loved or immensely loveable homes that buyers love — there's no limit to how much they will pay.

2. *Family-home buyers.* Buyers looking for a home for their families usually pay an excellent price. Of course, like all buyers, they hope to pay less. But when it comes to a choice between their love and their money, most focus on love.

3. *Market-price buyers.* Due to the self-interest and incompetence of so many agents, most buyers pay less than their maximum. Therefore, most homes are sold at what agents — and pundits — describe as 'market value'. Market price, however, is rarely the best price. It's like a wholesale price — and who wants to sell their home at wholesale?

4. *Bargain hunters.* Price is paramount to these buyers. If the price is low enough, they will buy any property. This group includes professional investors, property developers and those who haunt real estate auctions looking for properties to buy and flip.

# 157 What clues indicate that prospective buyers are interested?

If your price is low enough, many buyers will be interested. But the buyers likely to pay the best price are those who fall in love with your home. These are usually family home buyers.

If they are inexperienced, buyers often express joy as they view your home. They will find it hard to disguise their love of your home. Other buyers are more guarded.

But here are some signs that indicate their level of interest:

- If they speak about your home in the first-person possessive that's a sign of feeling ownership. For example, if they say, 'We will have to do a lot of work on this home,' the word 'we' indicates ownership. In their mind, it's already theirs. However, if they say, 'This place needs too much work', they're not using a possessive pronoun. Also, using crass words such as 'joint' or 'place' are not good signs. The best word to hear is 'home'.

- If children get excited, that's a good sign. Especially if they squeal with delight and yell, 'I want this room'. Or, 'Can this be my room, please, Mum?'
- The longer buyers spend at your home, the more interested they're likely to be.
- The more questions buyers ask that are specifically related to your home (not the general area), the more interested they are.
- If they praise some features or workmanship about your home and want more information, this is a great buying signal.
- If they spend more than 10 minutes in some part of your home — such as admiring a view — this augers well for a sale.
- If they whisper — in an excited manner — you are looking good.
- If they take photographs — especially after asking permission — that's another excellent sign.
- If they return for a second or third inspection, this shows positive interest.
- When they are leaving your home and they reach their car, if they turn back and spend more than a few seconds looking at your home, this is another excellent sign. They may be in love.

## A note of caution

Almost all buyers will thank you. Some will add flattery such as, 'You've got a lovely home'. This does not mean they want to buy your home. Many sellers get their hopes up when buyers offer praise. When nothing happens, the sellers blame the agent: 'What a hopeless salesperson to let those keen buyers slip away'.

If buyers want your home, your agent will soon let you know.

After inspections are over, no news is usually bad news.

# 158 How can prospective buyers be persuaded to pay a high price for my home?

One of the most attractive aspects of a home to most home buyers is an honest home seller. If buyers feel good about you, they will feel good about your home. An agent with high negotiation skills will almost certainly have high ethical standards. It's mostly cheats who are pushy and overly persuasive. They use their malevolent talents against you. If any agent suggests anything that may deceive buyers, you can be sure this agent will also deceive you. Agents are not prejudiced with deception. The bad ones deceive everybody. Even themselves.

Real estate agents with high negotiation skills have (or do) the following.

- *They qualify buyers.* Unless an agent knows the highest price a buyer can pay for a home, they can't get you the highest price for your home. The process of qualifying buyers is explained in question 162.
- *They show enthusiasm.* If an agent doesn't have a high opinion of your home, you won't get the highest price.
- *They are knowledgeable.* It's amazing how many agents think they can sell a home when they know little about that home. When it comes to *selling* homes, those with the most knowledge have the most power. And are most likely to get the best price.

- *They are positive.* Without being fake, a good agent will accentuate positive aspects of your home.
- *They neutralise negatives.* Often, what many buyers — and even owners — see as negative aspects of a home can be neutralised. There is no need to hide the (perceived) negatives of a home. The agent should understand that some negatives can become positives. For example, a home on the low side of the street is a positive to buyers who seek privacy. A home on a busy road may be a source of comfort to some buyers. And a home backing a railway line is exciting to men who loved trains as boys. The writer W Somerset Maugham often used idioms to describe a point. He would have said, 'One man's meat is another man's poison'. So, just because you don't like some aspect of your home it doesn't mean you need to sell it for thousands of dollars less than it's worth.
- *They know that one buyer is all you need.* This is one of the most overlooked facts in home selling. Agents constantly tell sellers to do something — often misleading — that will attract more buyers. Conversely, agents will often discourage home sellers from doing something — such as standing firm on the price — because it will attract fewer buyers. But how many buyers do you need to buy your home? A skilled negotiator understands this point.
- *They discover the buyer's main motive.* There are many reasons why the right buyer will fall in love with your home; but there is probably one major reason. In all the excitement, it's easy to forget this main reason. But a great negotiator never does. Every time the buyers ask for a discount or a concession, the agent will hammer the main motive and remind the buyers why they love the home.

# 159 What do I do if I have more than one serious interested party?

If you have more than one buyer interested in your home, this could be an excellent chance to sell for a much better price — provided your agent is a skilled negotiator. The agent should approach each buyer in private and discover the maximum price each will pay for your home. The agent needs to discover the buyers' 'walk-away-price' — not a bluff or an attempt to buy your property more cheaply.

The agent must know how to discover the buyers' highest price. A skilled agent will use a buyers' price declaration (see question 173).

The agent should be diplomatic and empathetic. Good negotiators do not upset buyers. They convey the fairness of the negotiation. Your agent is paid by you, which means your agent has a fiduciary duty to act in your best interests.

# 160 What are 'terms'? How do terms affect value?

One of the most underrated factors in the selling of a home is what's called 'terms'.

Terms can be anything from accepting a lower deposit or a delayed settlement; or allowing early access under a licence/rental agreement or agreeing to vendor finance (often a small percentage of the sale price), which is explained in the next question. From the buyers' perspective, terms might mean releasing their deposit to help the sellers finance their future, allowing the sellers to remain in occupation (for no or low rent) for a short period, and even purchasing household or personal items — from furniture to vehicles.

If you offer attractive terms, buyers will be less inclined to push you down in price. Indeed, many buyers pay extra for good terms. Don't fall for another absurdity of auctions where agents say you can lock buyers in on a contract under harsh terms. This can turn the best buyers away.

Find out what buyers want and see if you can offer appealing terms. You could be amazed at the power of attractive terms in increasing the value of your home. Many agents are not interested in negotiating terms — unless, of course, it makes the difference between a sale or no sale.

For the sellers, however, terms can work wonders. Instead of agreeing to drop your price, see what terms you can offer the buyers as an incentive to pay a better price

# 161 What is 'vendor finance'?

Many rural properties are sold with the assistance of vendor finance. This means the seller lends the buyer some money to assist with the purchase of the home.

If that sounds frightening or impractical, consider the following example.

## How vendor finance works

Let's say you want $3 million for your home. But confidentially, you'd accept $2.8 million. And let's say the agent gives you a firm offer of $2.7 million. Be sure to ask *why* the buyer wants a discount of $300 000. The agent may say that the buyers' financier will only grant funds to allow them to pay $2.7 million. This is what commonly happens. If they could pay more, many buyers would pay more. Sometimes the only thing stopping them is lack of finance. Yet they can comfortably afford repayments.

Maybe you come close to accepting the offer—especially as it's within 10 per cent of the asking price. And, to you, it's actually only $100000 below the price you would accept.

Forget the total price. It's easy to give away thousands of dollars when you're selling a home for millions of dollars. Focus on the amount you are asked to discount. That's $300000. Even $100000 is a lot of money—especially if you put it on your kitchen table. Consider how long it would take you to save $100000.

Rather than accept their offer of $2.7 million, ask if they are seriously wanting your home. If the agent confirms that they are serious, ask this question: 'If these buyers could borrow enough to give us the asking price of $3 million, would they do so?'

They should say yes.

So, instead of dropping $300000, offer to vendor finance them for $300000.

Better they owe you $300000 than you give it away.

The buyers can agree to pay you $30000 per year for 10 years—at no interest (even though most vendor finance comes with a modest interest rate).

This equates to $577.00 per week. Not bad compared to the zero dollars had you accepted the offer of $2.7 million.

You just turned a $300000 discount on your price into a $2500-per-month income for the next 10 years. Don't let the agents tell you this is too complicated. If the agents were going to receive $300000 over 10 years, they'd be interested.

Look after your money. Always consider vendor finance before dropping the price, especially if the stated reason for being asked to drop your price is the buyers' financial limitations.

Be sure you get competent independent legal advice and that you comply with all laws.

# 162 How does a skilled agent qualify buyers and discover their highest price?

Some agents are dreadful negotiators. They do more harm than good. They rarely discover the buyers' highest price.

The most basic principle of negotiation is this: if you want to find out what the other side is thinking, *ask them.*

Incredibly, many agents don't know how to discover the buyers' maximum price. Instead, these agents will make such pathetic comments to buyers as:

'Would you like to make an offer?'

Or 'Would you like to see how low I can get the seller to go?'

Or, worst of all, they will tell the buyers the lowest price they think the sellers will accept.

Such agents never know the buyers' highest prices.

A skilled agent spends time qualifying buyers.

In other words, a skilled agent knows the maximum amount that buyers will pay for any house. This is done by finding out the buyers' financial capability. And all qualifying takes place in comfortable and respectful surroundings. Not with the buyers sitting in a gutter or leaning against a fence or a car bonnet with an agent in sunglasses and a black suit yelling at them.

A skilled negotiator asks buyers what is most important to them: the quality of the home, or the price of the home. If the buyers say both — the price and the home — the agent may then ask, 'Given a choice between having a bargain or having a home where you will be happy for many years, which takes priority?'

Most buyers will prefer a home they love before a bargain. Oh sure, they like to buy a home they love at a bargain price. But they can only achieve this with agents who are not skilled negotiators.

If a skilled agent is qualifying them properly, most buyers will share their personal details because the agent is helping them with one of the most important decisions of their lives: a home for them and their family.

Believe it, respectful qualifying works.

But many agents rarely ask buyers any qualifying questions. They don't have time. They are running from one open house to another, sometimes meeting dozens (even hundreds) of people each week. How can they possibly identify the best buyers?

The only way this can be done is by qualifying. And the best way to qualify is to make sure that your agent is sitting in front of buyers who are likely to buy.

There are four stages in the selling process, one of which is qualifying buyers. These stages are perpetual:

- The first stage is speaking to prospects.
- The second stage is qualifying prospects.
- The third stage is presenting to qualified prospects.
- And the fourth stage is closing the sale.

Many agents go straight to the fourth stage: closing the sale. They don't qualify. They don't present. All they do is push sellers and buyers to sign contracts. That's not negotiating. That's high-pressure selling. Even bullying. Many agents make no attempt to get the best deal for the people paying their commissions: the home sellers.

In the real estate world, many sales contracts get signed when sellers crack and reveal their lowest price; not when buyers offer their highest price.

It's astounding how incompetent some agents are at negotiation. This is why if you are selling your home and you can't find a skilled negotiator as your agent, you are better off selling without an agent.

Do it yourself and be as much as hundreds of thousands of dollars in front.

# 163 Is a home only worth what a buyer is prepared to pay?

It is commonly accepted that a property is only worth what a buyer is prepared to pay for it. This is true with many agents, especially those who are not skilled negotiators.

But if you hire a good negotiator, it is more correct to say, *Your home is worth what a skilled agent can persuade a buyer to pay.* And that can be thousands of dollars more.

# 164 Is it greedy to want more than agents quote me?

It's human nature to want the best price for your biggest asset. But demanding a price way above market price can cause you to sell way below market price. And, given that many agents overquote the likely selling price, if you want more than agents are quoting, you probably don't want an agent — you want a magician.

There's a big difference between being financially prudent and being too optimistic (which agents call 'greedy'). Don't be too afraid of pricing your home too low because if you get more than one buyer — as often happens when a home is well priced — you could easily get more than you originally hoped to get. The price will rise as each buyer is required to offer their highest price (in private with a buyers' price declaration; see question 174).

Don't be silly and ask for more than you can possibly achieve — unless you're prepared to wait months, even years. Play it smart. Be realistic.

If you own shares in a public company that are valued (on the ASX) at $50 each and you try to sell them for $70, stockbrokers will laugh. Without realising it, this is what happens in the real estate market if sellers ask too much too soon. They end up getting too little too late, after their home has become a lemon.

So, be smart.

Start at a price that will attract more than one genuine buyer — and then, provided you have a skilled agent, watch the price rise.

# 165 Should buyers pay a deposit when they make an offer?

Yes. In most instances you should only consider offers that are accompanied by a deposit. The bigger the deposit, the more genuine the offer. Remember the movie where the character (a sports agent) yelled 'Show me the money!'? The same should apply with you. The best agents insist that buyers pay a deposit when making an offer.

Some buyers will promise to pay a deposit *if* their offer is accepted. The agent should tell the buyers that there is more chance of their offer being accepted if they pay a deposit *first*. And the bigger the deposit, the more chance their offer will be accepted.

Serious buyers make serious offers and pay serious money to show they're serious.

If a buyer makes an offer — and has not paid a deposit or even signed a contract at the offered price — and you accept the offer, the buyer then knows the price you are willing to accept. The buyer may then say, 'Okay, I'll think about it'. And then word spreads about the lesser amount you agreed to accept.

### Beware the 'try-on' offers

Some buyers make low offers on several properties without paying a deposit. If any sellers accept, the buyers nab a bargain at no risk to themselves.

These are 'try-on' offers.

So, how do you know if offers are serious?

The buyer pays a decent deposit.

# 166 What happens if buyers want to cut out the agent?

Be very careful of buyers suggesting that you cut out the agent—for two reasons.

1. *Real estate shoplifting.* If your agent is negotiating with buyers and you conspire with those buyers to cut out the agent, you will likely be sued. For the full commission.

   In addition to commission, you may incur hefty legal costs, both yours and the agents' costs (should you lose, which you almost certainly will).

Good agents who do well deserve to be paid. Even not-so-good agents should be paid for a good result. Don't cheat them.

Look at it this way: if you went to Bunnings and took a shovel without paying, you are a shoplifter. Shoplifters steal.

With agents you agree to pay for their service and, ostensibly, their skill. If you receive this service and don't pay, that's stealing too.

Don't become a real estate shoplifter. No matter how strong the temptation or justification.

2. *Cheats are cheats.* Real estate shoplifting often begins when buyers return to the home without the agent. They ask for another look. They say they only need a couple of minutes. It seems reasonable. They may say they can't contact the agent. 'He never answers his phone; we've left four messages.' Although these claims are likely untrue, they can be convincing. The sellers then allow the buyers into their home.

   Soon these sweet-sounding buyers reveal a darker side. They may lower their voices. A smile — more of a leer — appears. They suggest something that's 'good for you/good for me'.

   What are they saying? What's going on?

   Cut out the agent. That's what they are suggesting.

   If the commission is $100 000, the buyer tries to convince the seller that the agents deserve nothing. The two of them — buyer and seller — can share this commission. That's $50 000 each.

   But look out.

   Cheats are cheats. If they cheat the agent, you can be sure — given the first chance — they will cheat you too.

   Decent home sellers don't cheat, and they don't consider another dishonest ploy that not-so-decent sellers and buyers might try. These rogue sellers and buyers wait until the agent's agreement has ended and then get together and arrange a sale and avoid the commission. In such cases the agent is almost certainly able to claim the full commission. Plus, the agent's legal costs. Plus, their own legal costs. Plus, other penalties that can apply.

Dishonesty can be messy and nasty, as well as shameful.

# 167 Is it safe to sign an option?

Occasionally, some buyers ask sellers to sign an option agreement. This means that for a few dollars (often as little as $1000, which is generally non refundable) the sellers grant the buyers the exclusive rights to purchase their home at an agreed price within a certain time. At the end of the time, the buyers either exercise (go ahead with) the option or forfeit their option fee. While they may seem appealing, options can be dangerous for sellers, especially if their property is tied up for a long period, during which it can appreciate in value far in excess of the earlier agreed price. You should never sign an option (or any real estate related document) without getting legal advice — and that means getting legal advice from a lawyer with no connection to the agent or the buyer.

Beware of a suggestion that you use the same lawyer (or conveyancer) as the buyer because this saves time or because the lawyer understands the option method. In other words, the lawyer — who is almost certainly dodgy — understands how to look after the buyers. You need a lawyer who's independent of the buyers. A lawyer who looks after you and therefore works solely to protect your best interests.

Be careful. Some buyers offer an enormous price. But they ask for an option for a long time — as much as one or two years, sometimes longer. And they pay a minimal option fee, which is all they lose if they don't exercise the option. This could tie your property up for a long time with no benefit to you other than hope. Or you can claim the option fee, which could be as little as $1000 — or less.

Options are a favourite method of developers. The late Alan Bond was a notorious property developer. He loved buying with options. He once boasted that he could tie up multi-million-dollar properties for as little as $500 — especially with help from the sellers' agents (who are supposed to act in the sellers' best interests).

# 168 Is it good to sell to a property developer?

Sometimes. But be careful. Property developers are some of the smartest and most ruthless people in real estate. This is why they never sell by auction.

Developers are also among the most rapacious players in the industry. The reason they want your property is for profit.

Sometimes, agents and developers are in cahoots. Agents approach sellers on behalf of developers. But then the agents expect the sellers to pay a commission for selling to the developer. The developer should pay the commission. Especially if these agents push you down in price to curry favour with the developer.

Many developers promise agents the right to sell the completed development. Depending on what they build, the agent's ultimate commission could be millions of dollars.

The developer should either pay the agent's commission or undertake not to have any future commercial interest with the developer who buys your property.

There are some decent developers. So yes, it can be good to sell to a good one.

> ## The icing on the cake
>
> If dealing with developers, always try to 'get one' in addition to the agreed sale price. 'Get one' means getting one of whatever is going to be developed on the site. One apartment, one townhouse, one block of land. Whatever. If the developer is building, say, 50 apartments, they will often give you one on top of the purchase price. But you must ask.

# 169 What do I do if the buyer is using a buyers' agent?

Most buyers' agents are former sellers' agents. They know how easy it is to buy properties for less than market value. They know the tricks of the trade. They can save a buyer several hundred thousand dollars (even millions of dollars on high-end properties).

If your agent is not a skilled negotiator, there's an excellent chance that, to use a corny phrase, the buyers' agent will have them for breakfast.

However, if your agent is a skilled negotiator, it could become a gladiatorial battle between your agent and the buyers' agent.

Hopefully your agent will win, and you will get the highest possible price.

# 170 What do I do if I am pressured to make a counter-offer?

Getting involved in counter-offers is one of the surest ways to short-sell a property. No matter what offer you get, insist that the buyers sign a buyers' price declaration (see question 173).

Don't be shy about this. Being timid could cost you thousands of dollars.

Do what is best for you and your family: use a buyers' price declaration. If your agent doesn't know how to use such a declaration, your agent is not a skilled negotiator.

# 171 Should I sell to a home buyer or a property investor?

Always try and target the home buying market rather than the investment market.

Family home buyers buy with their hearts. Investors buy with their wallets.

The only time it may be appropriate to target investors is when you own a typical investment property that will not be attractive to home buyers.

The only sellers who actively target investors are spruikers selling massively overpriced properties to naïve investors. If you wish to buy an investment property it is safer to buy from a normal suburban agency. And avoid cookie-cutter properties (aka 'lookalikes').

# 172 How do I know if the price I'm being offered is the highest price buyers will pay?

The answer to this question is so simple, it's brilliant.

What's amazing, though, is that when this question is asked of agents, few can answer it satisfactorily. They'll splutter and stammer and change the subject or, like scared rabbits, retreat to their cliché burrows. They'll make meaningless comments in a desperate attempt to hide their ignorance. They'll mutter platitudes about 'the market' or how it 'depends on the day' — even saying that a home will need to 'value up', meaning that the buyers' lender will require the home to be valued. As if you, the sellers, need to be careful not to sell your home for too much.

But forget the nonsense. Reject agents who can't explain a simple method for ensuring that buyers offer their highest price.

The simple method for discovering a buyer's highest price was first explained by Michael Kies, Australia's best real estate teacher. Michael, who was formerly one of the most successful agents in Australia — both in quantity of results and quality of care — negotiated hundreds of sales. Very early in his career, he learned what all agents soon discover: that many buyers are bluffing when they say that their offer for a home is their maximum.

One day, after being told by some buyers that they 'wouldn't pay a cent more', Michael did what many agents do. He believed them. He then sold the home to another buyer who offered a better price.

The first buyers were furious. One was in tears. 'Why didn't you give us a chance to increase our offer?' she said.

Michael said, 'But you told me you wouldn't pay any more'.

They were bluffing.

As all agents know, the common 'buyers' bluff' often backfires on buyers. This happens when agents sell the home to another buyer for a higher price without telling the first buyer.

And then, when the first buyer says they would have increased their offer — after earlier declaring they couldn't/wouldn't pay more — the common agents' response is to use a hackneyed phrase: 'All buyers are liars'.

But in so many of these situations, the losing buyers aren't the only ones to lose out. The sellers get hurt too. They miss out on thousands of dollars because the agent didn't know how to test (or call) the buyers' bluff. Labelling buyers as liars is how agents deny their incompetence.

To prevent him from getting further abuse from buyers who were bluffing and, more importantly, to make sure his sellers definitely sold for the highest price on the day of sale, Michael Kies designed the buyers' price declaration (see question 173).

# 173 How does a buyers' price declaration work?

Instead of you making the common mistake of revealing your lowest price, the buyers are asked to reveal their highest price. The challenge is to stop the buyers bluffing. This is done by persuading the buyers to reveal the price above which they will no longer want to buy the home.

This is known as their 'walk-away price'.

The agent says to the buyers (politely), 'Please think about this carefully and let me know the highest price you are willing to pay. Please don't bluff because I am going to ask you to tell me — in writing — that you have truthfully made your best offer. And that, at any amount above the amount of your offer, you will definitely walk away. This is your walk-away price.

'If your offer is not accepted, then you will not object if I (on behalf of the owner) sell the home to another buyer at a higher price than you offered (which you have stated, in writing, is your best offer). You need to assure me that you will not pay one dollar more than the price you have declared.'

When buyers realise the seriousness and finality of the buyers' price declaration, many instantly increase their offer. Some offer thousands more than their original verbal offer. Unlike a public auction — where each buyer sees the amount that other buyers are offering — if there is more than one buyer, none are told what other buyers are offering.

Even if there are no other buyers, the buyers are still asked to declare their highest price.

This is how sellers get the best price.

## 174 Can I see a sample buyers' price declaration?

Sure, it's on the opposite page.

## 175 Is it true that increasing the price can be successful?

As crazy as it seems, increasing the asking price can sometimes succeed. The New York billionaire Michael Bloomberg reportedly said, 'When I am struggling to sell something, I mark it up not down. It works most times'.

In my real estate life and, more recently, in helping sellers through our vendor advocacy service, Jenman Support, I have used this technique. Sometimes, it works wonderfully. For example, a gorgeous property a couple of hours from Melbourne had been for sale for a year for $1.8 million. The price appeared too cheap, which made buyers wonder what was wrong with it. I suggested they increase the price. Within six months they were rejecting offers close to $3 million.

But to be sure, this technique is best for unique properties. Especially expensive ones. Such properties can sell for a difference of hundreds of thousands of dollars — even millions of dollars — depending on the buyer. A higher price on such homes can attract higher paying buyers.

# The Jenman Support Buyers' Price Declaration

1.  We have inspected the property located at:

........................................................................................................

*Address of Property*

2.  Following discussions with the seller's agent, we advise that we are **interested in buying the property** subject to any further independent advice which we may seek.

3.  The HIGHEST price we are prepared to pay for the property is...

..............................................................$..............................................

*Price to be written in words as well as in numbers*

4.  We also advise that should someone else offer a price for this property that is HIGHER than the price stated above (in Point 3), we will NOT increase our price. The price stated is the **Highest Price** we are prepared to pay.

5.  In order to demonstrate both the sincerity and the FINALITY of our price, we declare that we do NOT require notification should another buyer offer a price higher than that offered by us. In such event, we understand that the property may be immediately sold to the other buyer. We will NOT pay more than the price already stated, therefore we do not require an opportunity to increase our price.

6.  This declaration does not place any legal obligation upon us to purchase the property, even at the price stated above. **Until such time as a formal contract has been signed by both the seller and us, there is no legal obligation for us to buy or for the seller to sell.** We also understand that the amount of our maximum price will not be revealed to any person other than the agent and the seller.

Name: .....................................................................................

Signature: .......................................... Date:...........................

**By signing this declaration, I acknowledge that:**

  a. **I have been given a copy of it; and**

  b. **that I have been advised to seek independent advice.**

*Note:* If you intend to use this technique, you must be confident and able to justify your price increase. For example, if a property is like many others—such as in a housing estate or a block of apartments—increasing the price can make matters worse.

# 176 Is it better to sell a home vacant rather than occupied?

It depends on the home. If the home is beautiful and has a lovely atmosphere, it is better to sell it occupied. But if the home is scruffy and/or unclean, it should be vacant. Better to have a home vacant and clean than occupied and filthy.

If your home is vacant and clean, consider having it staged. See question 121.

# 177 How should I respond to the pressure of a deadline offer?

When you receive an offer with a deadline attached to it, you will probably feel stressed. A deadline is often one notch above a threat. You're being asked to decide in a hurry, often without having time to think it over. You're almost being bullied.

Unless you feel totally confident with a deadline offer, say no. Sure, you may have to accept a lower price later, but that's not what usually happens. Most deadline offers are below the highest value. The reason the buyers want you to act quickly is because they know they are getting a bargain. And they know that you will likely get a better offer later.

## Dismiss the stress

One seller was so stressed after receiving a deadline offer from an agent while she was driving that she pulled off the road feeling nauseous with anxiety. After getting advice, the lady dismissed the high-pressure agent. A month later, a better agent sold her home for $300000 more than the amount of the deadline offer.

## Key takeaways from part 9

- Just because you may be happy with a price, that doesn't mean it's the best price.
- Early offers are often the best offers you will ever receive. Consider them carefully.
- It's okay to want a high price, but if you hold out too long, you may sell too low.
- There are four 'types' of buyers. The best is the heart buyer. The worst is the bargain hunter.
- Learn to spot signals that indicate buyers are genuinely interested in your home.
- What may seem negative to some people can be positive to others. Focus on the positives.
- If more than one buyer likes your home, a skilled agent will get you the best price.
- Terms can be as important as price. Attractive terms can create a higher sale price.
- Instead of dropping your price, consider offering cash-strapped buyers vendor finance.

*(continued)*

- Agents who competently and politely qualify buyers discover their highest price.
- Agents who are good negotiators ask buyers to pay a substantial deposit with an offer.
- Don't sign an 'option' (or any document) without getting independent legal advice.
- Agents who have developers as buyers are often working for the developers.
- If buyers are using a buyers' agent, be sure your sales agent is a skilled negotiator.
- Learn how a buyers' price declaration works. It takes mere seconds to discover that you can sell your home for thousands of dollars more than you would otherwise have received.
- Don't play a counter-offer game. Instead, insist that your agent uses a buyers' price declaration.
- Family-home buyers generally offer much better prices than bargain-hunting investors.
- Sometimes it can be effective to increase your price (and drop your agent).
- Don't allow yourself to be stressed (or bullied) by an offer with a deadline.
- Be firm, but respectful and considerate in your dealings. Happy buyers pay more.

# PART 10

# CONQUERING YOUR SELLING WORRIES

Selling a home creates high anxiety for the seller. Rarely does everything go smoothly.

Many sellers encounter three major stress factors. First, their home is not as well accepted as they hoped. Agents constantly ask sellers to lower their price expectations. Second, most sellers are shocked at how much money they are asked to pay in marketing costs. And third, a series of go-wrongs increase stress levels.

It's not uncommon for sellers to experience 'seller fatigue'. They get so tired of bad news, high costs and low offers that they crack and undersell their homes just to relieve the stress. This applies mostly to inexperienced sellers, those who have not taken the time to learn how to sell for the highest price with the lowest stress.

In this part, you will see how to conquer common selling troubles. You will learn how to keep yourself positive and confident.

The more you know about how to sell well, the less stress you will feel.

Indeed, as many successful sellers attest: when you know how to handle agents — and buyers who want to pay less than the price you want — you will feel happy as well as confident.

Selling a home can be enjoyable and uplifting, especially when you save in expenses and when you sell your home for the best market price.

# Questions in this part

178.  If my home has not sold, is it my fault?

179.  What happens if offers are below the agent's quote?

180.  Why is false quoting so common and how does it work?

181.  After price, is there another big reason a home may not sell?

182.  What happens if buyers want a discount due to faults in my home?

183.  What happens if prospective buyers get a bad building report?

184.  How should I handle negative comments about my home?

185.  When should I drop my price?

186.  Does it look bad to prospective buyers if I switch agents?

187.  If an agent says, 'There are no buyers', is that ever true?

188.  What can I do if the buyers' lender values my home lower than the quoted price?

189.  If I can't get my price, should I wait until the market improves?

190.  If my home is not selling, should I withdraw it?

191.  What do I do if I'm sick of selling, but I want to sell?

192.  My home is better than others selling for the same or more, so why has mine not sold?

193.  What happens when nothing happens?

194.  What happens if I change my mind and decide to stay?

195.  What causes prospective buyers to reject a home?

196.  Who do I complain to if I'm unhappy with an agent?

197.  How do I know if an offer is a real offer or a dummy?

# 178 If my home has not sold, is it my fault?

There are two main reasons why homes may take a long time to sell: the price and the agent. For unique or high-end homes, time can also be a factor as they may need more time on the market. This could mean that the sellers may just have to wait for the right buyer to come along. Occasionally, high-end homes can sit on the market for months and then, suddenly, two different buyers appear at the same time — which means the sellers' despair can turn to delight.

Of course, when homes seem to be sitting idle with nothing happening the home sellers always blame the agents, labelling them as incompetent. And the agents always blame the sellers, labelling them as greedy.

But some sellers are incredibly stubborn. No matter how competent the agent or how long the property has been for sale, they refuse to accept that their price is too high. And yet, most of these sellers are not greedy. They are the victims of what is known as 'the endowment effect': the tendency to cling to possessions due to sentimentality. If owners wait long enough, most eventually get their price. The question of course is 'how long?' As an agent, I often quipped to stubborn sellers, 'Mr and Mrs Seller, the price you want is so high that the buyer for your home has probably not been conceived yet'.

All agents face a similar problem with stubborn sellers who refuse to lower their price. The tragic part is that many times the sellers sack their agent and go to a second agent only to sell for much less than they could have received with the first agent. This is one of the biggest mistakes sellers make. Realise this point: all agents want to sell your home. Even the worst agents need commission to survive. And if they don't make sales, they don't get commission. Very few agents will deliberately not sell your home.

If your property is not selling, the agent has worked hard and all the buyers in the area have been made aware of your property (and many have inspected it), and despite all of this, it hasn't sold, you only have two choices: lower your asking price or wait it out.

# 179 What happens if offers are below the agent's quote?

There is often a difference between an agent's quote prior to listing a home and the final selling price. Sometimes massively so.

Many agents will claim to be heroes when a market is booming. When prices subside, the same agents will blame the sellers for not 'listening to the market'.

When the agent gives you a quote before you list with them, you need to ask, quite firmly, if this quote is inflated. They will probably mutter something about 'letting the market decide'.

All agents should know their local market. Most do, but they are afraid to tell you the truth because you may reject them. If an agent assures you that they are not inflating their quoted sale price to win your listing, ask if they will consider discounting or even forfeiting their commission if they later ask you to sell below the price they're quoting. Most will go into near apoplexy.

If you want to soften your request, ask this question: 'Below what price will you charge us no commission?'

As most homes sell below the agent's initial quote, always consider this question (when the time comes): 'If you're asking us to drop our selling price, surely it's only fair that you drop your commission too?'

# 180 Why is false quoting so common and how does it work?

Most agents (about 90 per cent) participate in false quoting. Without false quoting, these agents would struggle to find houses to sell, and they would struggle to find buyers for those houses.

Even the most honest agents get snared in the nefarious practice of false quoting. It's built into the systems and methods that most agents feel they are forced (or instructed) to use. The way they see it, they have no choice. Quote honestly and lose. Quote falsely and win. Lie or die. That's the sad and tragic reality of real estate for agents in the 21st century.

False quoting has become so ubiquitous in real estate that, rather than complaining about it, sellers and buyers need to learn how to deal with it.

But first, it's important to understand false quoting — why it happens and how it works.

There are two types of false quotes.

## *False overquoting to sellers — why and how*

Finding homes for sale (listings) is the major focus of agents. Without good listings, agents can't make sales. But the competition to win listings is fierce.

Most agents know that, generally, the agent who quotes the highest estimate of the value of a home wins the listing. Quite simply, most sellers reward agents for lying to them.

The biggest (and best) liars therefore list the most homes.

But, once agents list homes, their next challenge is to sell those homes.

And because they have overquoted the likely selling price, their major focus is now to get the owner to reduce the asking price.

Of course, after they win listings, agents can't say to the sellers: 'We lied to you about the likely selling price of your home. We did this so that we could sign you up and tie you down for four months. And now we start to talk you down in price. In the industry, it's called "conditioning". So, brace yourself for what's about to come'.

No, agents need to be more subtle if they intend to turn those listings into sales.

Enter the great alibi of so many dodgy agents: 'the market'.

From now on, the most common words sellers will hear are 'the market'.

'We will take the property to the market.'

'We will see how the market responds.'

'We will give you the market feedback.'

'The market is getting tough.'

'You need to listen to the market.'

'The market says your property is only worth $…'

Can you see what's happening? The agents tell the lies. The market becomes their alibi.

Let's use an example. Say a home is genuinely worth about $2 million. To win the rights to sell that home — get the listing — agents overquote the likely selling price. The home will probably come on the market with the owners expecting as much as $2.4 million.

But now the agent must attract buyers to a home that's overquoted by at least $400 000. If the agent promotes the property at the price quoted to the sellers — $2.4 million — there will be no interest.

It's time to start underquoting to the buyers. Time to draw in a crowd. Time to 'take the property to the market'.

## False underquoting to buyers — why and how

In our example above, the agent now tells the sellers that, to attract buyers, it will be necessary to promote the home at a lower price.

If the sellers baulk, the agent will say that, at $2.4 million, there won't be any buyers. 'We need to get lots of buyers. When they fall in love with the home, we get them to compete. We talk them up in price.'

If the sellers still seem sceptical, the agent may say, with great sincerity, 'Trust me, I have been doing this a long time. This is how we get you the best price'.

Even though the sellers have reservations, most go along. They allow the agents to market their home at a lower price — usually within a price range.

In this case the agent might say $1.7 million to $1.87 million.

Now, when the crunch comes, the owners may agree to accept $2 million (the real value) or less — especially after they have been subjected to weeks of conditioning.

The agent says they are complying with the law (which requires them to quote within a range of 10 per cent of what they have told the owners). So, while they may verbally have said $2.4 million, when it comes to writing the price on their Listing Agreement, they adjust it down. It's a strategy to get the home sold (at any price).

It's amazing how many sellers swallow this sophistry.

So what is the buyers' response?

Ask any experienced home buyers — those who've been in the market for more than a few weeks — how they deal with the ubiquity of false quotes.

The typical buyers' response to the false quoting epidemic creates another dilemma, which makes it near impossible for even well-meaning agents to remain honest.

To protect themselves from disappointment and needless costs, many buyers add between 10 per cent and 20 per cent to the price they see quoted for a property.

So, if an honest agent — who's truthfully told the owners that their home is worth around $2 million (and the owners believe the honest agent) — promotes the home for $2 million, the buyers (who have become conditioned to being deceived) will believe the owners want between $2.2 million (10 per cent more) and $2.4 million (20 per cent more).

And what will happen then?

The home will be ignored. The buyers won't believe they are seeing a truthful quote. The home will become stale — even turned into a lemon. The honest agent will be punished for not underquoting — because most buyers know that most agents underquote. It's a real estate catch-22.

So, if the honest agent wants to sell a home for the genuine price of $2 million (or maybe a bit more), the agent will have no choice. They must compete in a dishonest market where most (at least 90 per cent) of homes are underquoted. If they are to get any enquiry for the home — assuming of course that they will first do what all good agents do and make a concerted attempt to speak with buyers known to them — they must underquote the home.

This is the real estate industry in Australia in the 2020s. Agents feel they must overquote the selling price to win sellers and then must underquote the selling price to attract buyers.

Honest agents truly despair. As do I. That's why I've written this book.

# 181 After price, is there another big reason a home may not sell?

Homes are like people. Those that are shunned are those that lack warmth and character. Some are just unappealing. If your home does not have a good feel, it will be hard to find a good buyer, let alone get a good price.

Banal homes must compete with other banal homes. The buyers are not looking for the nicest homes, just the cheapest homes. The sellers who accept the lowest prices win the buyers.

Some homes are so badly lacking in character, they sit on the market for months. They become stale, rejected and scorned. These homes should only be placed on the market during a frantic boom when buyers will buy almost anything because of the lack of available homes for sale.

# 182 What happens if buyers want a discount due to faults in my home?

Most faults with your home should be either visible or disclosed (if you are aware of them). If you have already adjusted your price downwards to make allowance for these faults then, hopefully, the buyers will not ask for a discount (as you've already given it). If you are trying to sell a home with faults for the price of a similar home without faults, perhaps it may be fair to offer a discount if asked.

Once the sale price has been agreed — and prior to the sale becoming legally binding — the buyers can only reasonably request a discount if they discover faults that were not visible (or known) to them when they inspected the home. This often occurs when buyers arrange a building inspection report.

Do what's fair. But remember, if buyers love a home, it's like loving a person: they tend to overlook (or forgive) faults, as my wife does with me!

## 183 What happens if prospective buyers get a bad building report?

Most building reports are 'bad'. That's how they are supposed to be. They are an exercise in fault finding. No matter how small the faults, they will likely be included in the building inspection report.

For inexperienced buyers, a building report can be terrifying. Often, it's enough to make them cancel their purchase. But unless the report reveals major faults not visible or not known to the buyers *before* they agreed to buy, a good agent should convince them to go ahead with the sale.

To lessen the chance of losing a sale due to a 'bad building report', consider obtaining a building report at your expense before you list your home for sale. And then openly make this report available to interested buyers and discuss any points of concern.

One of the worst things you can do is cover up faults — or hope the buyers don't notice something. This can lead to major distrust.

The better you treat the buyers, the better your chance of the best result.

## 184 How should I handle negative comments about my home?

When you get negative comments — or 'market feedback', as agents love to call it — about your home, the first question to ask is this: Are the comments genuine? If so, are they legitimate or frivolous? Worse, are they fake — in other words, part of an agent's conditioning process?

The golden rule with negative comments is not to let them get you down. Negative comments can be like psychological torture. Such negativity is often pre-planned. It's designed to make you crack and lower your price expectations. It may not be pleasant, but it is the reality of modern real estate. So much of what many agents do is designed to condition sellers.

A great question to ask of agents or buyers is, 'Do I need to know this information?' This is particularly relevant if the subject of the negative comments is visible. For example, if your home only has two bedrooms and you get lots of comments saying it only has two bedrooms, then you are not being told anything not openly disclosed. Don't be bullied. Simply ask why the buyers are looking at your two-bedroom home if they want more than two bedrooms.

The most common negative comment will be that your price is too high. There are many ways of handling this comment; one of the best is to ask the agent why they showed your home to people who can't afford it. Maybe the buyers should look in a cheaper area. Such a quip may dent the buyers' ego and cause them to pay your price.

If buyers knock your house too much, it doesn't mean you have the wrong house — it means they are the wrong buyers for your house.

They are not buyers, they are knockers.

# 185 When should I drop my price?

Picture your home's price like a mountain. Highest price at the top. Lowest price at the base.

At the base, there are dozens of buyers who will gladly buy your home at the bargain price. The higher you go on the price mountain, the fewer buyers you find. To achieve the best price, you need to start near the top of the mountain and work your way down until you find the highest buyer.

The trouble for many sellers is knowing when to move down the price mountain.

Let's say your home is worth somewhere around $2 million. And let's say you hired a valuer who confirmed that your home should sell for $2 million.

It's not unusual for homes worth $2 million to be on the market for as much as $2.5 million.

But if there is no interest at that level, it can be dangerous to leave your home at that price for too long. As already mentioned, the longer a home is on the market, the greater the danger of underselling.

It's important to be pragmatic and realistic.

So, while it's okay to start trying to sell your home for a price that's at — or close to — the top of the mountain, it's not okay to get 'stuck' there.

> *Don't be scared of going too low with your asking price. If you attract more than one buyer, the price can often start climbing back up the mountain.*

Here are 12 indicators that it may be time to drop your price.

1. Your agent shows you a list of all interested buyers they've dealt with and can tell you what has happened with each buyer after follow-up and feedback.
2. Your agent has given your 'love list' to all buyers.
3. If your property is suitable for investors, your agent has contacted (spoken with) landlords for whom they currently manage properties to see if they are interested.

4.  Your agent has shown you details of other homes similar to yours that have sold. *However*, be sure they sold recently (while your home has been for sale). Markets can change quickly.

5.  If there are any buyers still interested, your agent has considered using enticing terms. As the saying goes, 'Think outside the box'. Good sales can be made when good terms are offered. See question 160 for a reminder of how effective terms can be.

6.  If there are any buyers who've said that your home is slightly above their price range, you have offered them vendor finance if possible (see question 161).

7.  You've invested in a registered valuation to be sure that you are realistic with your asking price.

8.  You've checked the hidden search price for your home and have confirmed that it's not underquoted.

9.  Your advertisement does not contain too much information. It cannot be overstressed: the purpose of an advertisement is to attract enquiries, not to sell the home.

10. Your home is clean and well-presented. Any necessary improvements to lift the value have either been done or are being considered. This includes the possibility of staging. See question 123 for examples of how staging can help to sell a home.

11. If you have any doubts about the agent, you have had someone mystery-shop the agent and confirm that your home is being spoken about with enthusiasm (see question 34).

12. You have made sure that your home is not overadvertised. If your home is 'everywhere', buyers may think something is wrong with it.

Although it can cause you gut-wrenching pain to drop your price, when you eventually sell and move on with your life, you will be so glad you have sold. And, if you had a good agent, you would have sold for the best market price.

Ask yourself another question: How can you do better than the best?

# 186 Does it look bad to prospective buyers if I switch agents?

It is unlikely that buyers will think badly of you (or your home) if you switch agents. On the contrary, if you switch from an incompetent agent to a competent agent, the buyers will likely respect you. Especially if your second agent works harder. Buyers appreciate agents who work hard and follow them up. There is nothing wrong with replacing a slack agent with an active agent. It's usually the right move.

# 187 If an agent says, 'There are no buyers', is that ever true?

This is a common statement made by agents when times are tough. Like most real estate clichés, it's nonsense. There are always buyers around — if prices are low enough.

A good question to ask an agent who says there are no buyers around is, 'What would happen if your current listings were half price?'

They'd all be sold immediately.

But didn't you say there were no buyers around? ☺

# 188 What can I do if the buyers' lender values my home lower than the quoted price?

This is a problem faced by many sellers. They think they've got a great sale and then, suddenly, their property is valued below the sale price. The bank then refuses to lend as much as the buyers need.

You have four choices in such circumstances:

1. Wait for another buyer who can pay the same high price and obtain finance. But you risk the same problem again.
2. Consider vendor finance for the shortfall — although the bank may not allow a second loan/mortgage.
3. Reduce your price expectations, especially if the high price you are asking is unlikely to happen soon. This could mean selling to the existing buyers for the most they can afford.
4. Withdraw your property from sale and wait until the market improves.

# 189 If I can't get my price, should I wait until the market improves?

Many frustrated sellers who can't get the price they want say they will wait until the market improves.

But how long are they prepared to wait? Months? Years?

Here's the problem most people face: if they're buying another home in a more expensive area, then, if the price of their own home goes up, so does the price of the home they want to buy. Mathematically this can put them further behind.

Price rises are rarely confined to one area. If your home rises in value, so does everyone else's.

No-one can pick the top (or bottom) of any market. Some sellers who wait for the market to go up are shocked when it goes down. They sell for less than they could have achieved earlier.

Some sellers must consider this question: Should they sell or stay? These are often their only choices. Waiting for prices to increase rarely works — especially if you're selling your family home. Do what makes you happiest.

# 190 If my home is not selling, should I withdraw it?

When a property is not selling and the owners refuse to acknowledge that price is the major problem, some take the property off the market. They intend to re-list later — perhaps in another season. Unless the market is increasing rapidly — such as in a mad boom — this strategy rarely works. If price is the problem today, price will be the problem tomorrow. Taking a home off the market can exacerbate the problem.

And besides, if you withdraw your home from sale — when you really want to sell it — you give yourself no chance of selling. What's the point?

Don't think that if you withdraw and re-list later, that buyers won't catch on. With the lack of privacy these days, it's hard to conceal anything from anyone.

Although some people may disagree, it is usually better to leave your unsold property on the market and ride out any criticism than take it on and off the market.

Just because your home may have been for sale for a long time it does not always mean you will damage the value. Especially if you have a beautiful or unique home. In such cases you may just have to wait for the right buyer.

If your home is similar to many others, you may have to wait for the market to catch up to your price. And if you plan to buy elsewhere, this strategy may be self-defeating because, if you are up-trading, the price of your next house will also rise. This will put you in a worse position than if you had sold now.

# 191 What do I do if I'm sick of selling, but I want to sell?

Okay, you are fed up with keeping your home clean. And you don't want to reduce your asking price. Let's say you have tried everything from sprucing up your home — perhaps even some costly renovations. Your entrance looks superb. You have reduced your asking price several times. You are now on your fourth agent. Nothing seems to work. The agents keep asking you to lower your price. Is there anything else you can do?

Yes.

If you don't want to reduce your price — and you are tired of being the unsold home in your area — but you'd still be willing to sell when (maybe 'if') your definition of the 'right buyer' comes along, here's what to do.

Convert your Sole Agency listing (with one agent) to a 'bottom drawer listing' (with as many agents in your area as possible who agree to accept it).

Here's what you say to them. And be confident and positive — take control:

'We are sick of waiting. Please keep our property in mind and remember, when a buyer contacts you looking for a property that matches ours, call us and arrange an inspection. We will sign up with you for that buyer. And this way, we both might win because we'll both get a sale'.

Of course, you will only sign up for a matter of days (maybe 24 to 48 hours). The agents can literally keep your details in the bottom drawer of their desks. If they come across a buyer whose requirements match your home, then you may get your sale.

What have you got to lose? You win if the right buyer appears.

If there are a dozen agents in your area, most should agree to keep your property in mind — in other words, to have it as a 'bottom drawer listing'.

# 192 My home is better than others selling for the same or more, so why has mine not sold?

Well clearly, the buyers don't agree with you.

As tough as it may be, you must face facts.

All of us feel that our homes, our areas, our cars, our children, are valuable. We overestimate the worth of our assets, especially our homes. If we have lovingly owned them for years, it can be depressing when buyers don't feel the same.

How long are you prepared to wait? In the United States it's not uncommon for homes to be on the market for a year or more. Sometimes several years. This trend seems to be catching on in Australia.

The question we should all ask is, 'What's more important: our money or our happiness?' If you must lower your price and sell now, can you still do what you plan to do? If you will be happier, surely the right thing to do is sell now.

And remember this: if you lower your price, say, from $2 million to $1.6 million, you haven't lost $400 000, as some sellers bemoan. Your home was only worth $1.6 million. You can't lose what you never had.

Happiness should be your main goal; not a 2036 price in 2026.

# 193 What happens when nothing happens?

If your home is priced well and has been on the market and nothing is happening, it could simply mean that there is no suitable buyer for your home … at the moment.

As mentioned in question 178, sometimes you just have to wait for the right buyer to come along. This is particularly true with rare or unique properties. Such properties have a limited market.

Another alternative is to drastically reduce the price (below market value). But this is unpleasant and possibly unnecessary. If you can afford to hang on, do so. Wait it out. Provided, of course, that you are not unrealistic about your price. If you trust your agent, be guided by their advice.

If you don't trust your agent, consider interviewing other agents. Make it clear that you're not interested in just slashing the price or wasting thousands of dollars on needless advertising.

See if there is anything else an agent can do to entice the right buyer.

Consider target marketing. This means that you figure out who are the most likely buyers and where they can be found. And then tell your agent to contact these prospects directly. It's hard work. But hard work often pays off.

Start making outbound calls instead of waiting for incoming calls.

# 194 What happens if I change my mind and decide to stay?

It depends on what you signed and when. If you have signed up with an agent but haven't sold yet — and you deleted the nasty clauses in their Listing Agreement — you should be able to withdraw from selling with no cost, no penalty and no further obligation. If you didn't delete the nasty clauses, you could be charged thousands of dollars.

If you signed a contract to sell at an agreed price to specific buyers, it may be hard to stop the sale. Get immediate legal advice.

# 195 What causes prospective buyers to reject a home?

There are several reasons why buyers will reject homes — either before or after inspecting them.

Here are some of the more common reasons.

- Before inspecting:
  - *Being unable to inspect at a convenient time for the buyer.* This happens constantly when homes are only open for inspection for a few minutes each week.
  - *Being unable to contact the agent.* Be sure your agent promotes an office phone number and not just the number for an individual agent. Don't hire agents who are hard to contact. Mystery-shop agents before you choose one.
  - *Trying to 'sell' via an advertisement.* Too many sellers give away too much information in advertisements. This can make buyers reject a home because they make a false assumption about it. Don't try and *sell* using an ad.

- After inspecting:
  - *Feeling deceived.* Photoshopped images of your home that make it look like a movie star's mansion can work against you. Professional photography can trick buyers. They are lured by the gloss and glamour. And then they see the truth. They feel deceived and resentful. This causes them to walk away in disgust.
  - *Lacking cleanliness.* Don't confuse messy with dirty. Most lived-in homes have an element of mess about them. That's to be expected. It's dirt — and bad odours — that causes buyers to reject homes.
  - *Disliking the owners or agents.* It's amazing how many agents create unnecessary friction between sellers and buyers. This is especially true during a negotiation. If the buyers resent the way they are treated, they will often walk away. Treat buyers with respect and you'll increase your chances of selling your home to them.

# 196 Who do I complain to if I'm unhappy with an agent?

It can be so frustrating. An agent treats you badly. You decide to complain. But to whom?

Most people go to the Real Estate Institute without realising that the institute's aim is to protect real estate agents.

Many unhappy sellers and buyers try to leave a negative review on RateMyAgent only to discover that negative reviews are almost impossible to upload. The site is funded by real estate agents. It should be known as FakeMyAgent.

If the agent belongs to a network, you could complain to the network's head office. Such complaints are often buried or tossed in the too-hard basket. At best you may get an arrogant reply telling you that most customers are happy. You will be made to feel like a difficult customer, a whinger. The major aim of most networks is to protect and promote their brand.

Unless you've inserted a condition in the agent's listing contract allowing you to sack the agent in the event of unethical conduct, you will be unlikely to get satisfaction by complaining to the offending agent. You'll either be told to read the listing contract, or you will be threatened with legal action.

There are three places where you may get redress or share your bad experiences with others. First, your state government's Fair Trading or Consumer Affairs department. The Department of Fair Trading in NSW is the only state regulatory body to name businesses that receive multiple complaints each month. Big-name agents regularly feature in the list of most-complained-about companies.

Second, a Google review. Google reviews are not under the direct control of agents. Be wary of agents who don't have a Google page. The reason is likely because they want to prevent negative reviews being posted. That's why they stick with RateMyAgent, where most negative reviews from consumers are not allowed.

And third, consult a solicitor. You may discover that the agent has breached many consumer — even criminal — laws. A strong letter from a lawyer is often enough to get you at least an offer of compensation. Be careful. Never make threats such as, 'If you don't pay me, I will hurt you [in any form]'. You may commit a criminal offence. As with all serious happenings, get good legal advice.

Most agents don't understand the immense power of word-of-mouth advertising. Unhappy customers tell family, friends and colleagues. The reason so many agents are chronically short of listings is because people who deal with these agents rarely sing their praises. Many agents would rather build their personal profile than build their client service.

# 197 How do I know if an offer is a real offer or a dummy?

Ask the agent for the names and details of the alleged buyers.

Better still, tell the agent that you refuse to consider any offer unless the buyers pay a deposit as a show of good faith.

## Key takeaways from part 10

▶ If your home is not selling, you generally have two choices: lower the price or wait.

▶ If agents ask you to drop your price, ask them to drop their commission.

▶ If agents ask you for more advertising money, ask them to follow up more leads.

▶ False quoting is widespread. Don't complain about it. Learn how to handle it.

▶ Asking a lower (truthful) price can attract multiple buyers and increase your price.

▶ Reducing the asking price is *not* 'losing money'. You can't lose what you never had.

▶ Don't threaten agents if you are unhappy with them. Be polite and firm.

▶ If your agent is incompetent, sack them and hire a better agent.

▶ To complain about an agent, contact government departments, not real estate institutes.

▶ RateMyAgent makes it hard to leave negative reviews; use Google reviews instead.

(continued)

- ▶ Withdrawing your home for sale means you have no chance of selling.
- ▶ If you don't sell—and you hired an ethical agent—you will lose nothing. If not, you will likely lose thousands of dollars. If you protest, you may be sued.
- ▶ No matter what you hear, there are rarely 'no buyers around'.
- ▶ Consider asking several agents to accept a 'bottom drawer' listing (see question 191).
- ▶ If your home seems better than other homes selling faster at good prices, understand this tough truth: buyers do not agree with your opinion of your home.
- ▶ Understand the main reasons buyers reject homes for sale (see question 195).
- ▶ Buyers who 'knock' your home are rarely buyers. They are knockers.
- ▶ If you suspect an offer is not genuine, ask for details of the so-called buyers.
- ▶ Sometimes you may just have to wait for the right buyer.
- ▶ Keep your hopes up. The right buyer will likely come along.

# PART 11

# COMPLETING THE SALE

Once you (or your competent and ethical agent) have found the right buyer for your home — and the cooling-off period (if applicable) has expired — not much can go wrong. From now on, it's almost certainly plain selling (pun deliberate!). Your home has almost certainly been sold, and you are almost certain to get your money within the time stipulated in your sale contract.

But please note the words in the above paragraph: 'not much' and 'almost certainly'. And please remember that, in real estate, *nothing is definite until your sale has settled* (meaning you've got the buyers' money, and they've got your house).

In this part, you'll see that, after the sale, 'go-wrongs' are rare but not impossible. To ensure your peace of mind, it's important to know what could go wrong, no matter how unlikely.

But please remember, it's also important not to stress or worry too much about events that are highly unlikely to happen. The stoic philosophy teaches us that almost everything we worry about in life has already happened or, as with selling a home, is unlikely to ever happen. However, as any Boy Scout or Girl Guide will surely tell you: 'be prepared'.

As you'll learn in this part, you can eliminate the risk of some of the worst 'go-wrongs' by deleting any nasty clauses in an agent's Selling Agency Agreement.

Always remember that you are the boss. You are hiring an agent. You can — and should — set the conditions under which you employ an agent. Make sure you are firm, fair and friendly.

The most important factor for the prevention of 'after sale' trouble is to be firm before the sale.

## Questions in this part

198. When does the agent receive their commission?
199. What could delay settlement?
200. What happens if settlement is delayed?
201. What could cause a sale to fall through?
202. What happens if a sale falls through?
203. Will my selling agent help me buy another home?
204. What happens if I can't find a new home before settlement?

# 198 When does the agent receive their commission?

In most cases agents receive their commission at the same time as you receive the settlement money for the sale of your home. The agents usually hold the buyer's deposit (10 per cent or sometimes 5 per cent of the sale price) in their trust account. When the sale has been finalised ('settled'), the buyer's legal representative (or conveyancer) will issue what's called an 'order on the agent' instructing the agent to pay the deposit monies to the sellers after deducting their agreed agency commission and any other agreed expenses.

Please note (if you haven't already realised it): most sellers do not pay agents from their own personally held funds. The commission and any costs are deducted from the sale price. As one property specialist, David Kaity, openly and honestly admits: 'The large cost of using agents is disguised. The cost — however horrendous — comes out of the equity in the property. Sellers never see the money they pay to their agent and so they don't feel the pain of paying it'.

Be sure, therefore, that you always consider all money involved in the sale of your home — from the sale price to the commission to the myriad of costs — as being in 'isolation'.

No matter how small an individual expense may seem (in relation to the sale price), think of that money on its own. Let's say that you are charged $250 as an 'administration fee'. Such costs are often, at best, a 'try-on' and, at worst, a rip-off. On its own $250 is a lot of money. It may buy you a candlelit dinner with your loved one.

# 199 What could delay settlement?

The most common reason for a delay in the settlement of a sale is because the buyers are having difficulty arranging finance.

Other reasons could be if the financier insists on a new condition being met (such as mortgage insurance). Or if the buyers or sellers get sick or have an accident.

Sometimes the buyers might discover something about the home that was not disclosed prior to the purchase (and which, had it been disclosed, would have had a large impact on their decision to buy the home). These properties are euphemistically known as 'stigmatised homes'.

## Be an honest seller

A notorious example was the Gonzales family murders in 2001 in North Ryde. The home eventually sold in 2004. But the first the buyers heard about the triple murders was when they saw a news headline that screamed, 'Death House Sold!' They refused to buy the home, so they lost their deposit. After much intense wrangling and media publicity, my wife (Reiden Jenman) managed to have the buyers' deposit returned to them.

Since then, laws have been strengthened and buyers are more likely to ask probing questions, the most important of which (and which should always be asked) is the seven-word safety question: *Is there anything else we should know?* Always disclose anything you feel may negatively impact a buyer. As well as disclosing what you are legally required to disclose (such as a brutal murder), also consider disclosing what you feel should be ethically disclosed (such as a toxic neighbour). Although real estate brings out the worst in some people, don't be one of them. Treat buyers well and you may be surprised how well they treat you.

# 200 What happens if settlement is delayed?

Only about one in 100 sales are seriously delayed. And most delays are caused by buyers. Some buyers do not have pre-approval for their finance. They may have been pressured or rushed into signing a sales contract before receiving proper finance approval. Or they may have been given a verbal assurance that finance would be okay, but this was later withdrawn or disputed. In such cases, the sellers may issue the buyers a Notice to Complete (this is usually a demand to settle within 14 to 28 days). The sellers may also decide to charge (and the buyers agree to pay) penalty interest for their delay. According to legal experts, on a million-dollar home, this could amount to between $500 and $1000 per day. That's a strong deterrent against deliberately delaying a sale.

# 201 What could cause a sale to fall through?

Once the cooling-off period (if applicable) has passed, sales almost never fall over. Estimates are that about one in every 2500 fail to settle with the same buyers and sellers. The reasons are also rare and therefore largely unforeseen, such as the death of one or more sellers or buyers. Or the property is razed in a fire. So don't be overly anxious — it would be very unlucky for you to be the one in 2500.

# 202 What happens if a sale falls through?

If the buyers fail to settle, the sellers may be entitled to keep the buyers' deposit (usually 10 per cent of the sale price). But, as well as forfeiture of their deposit, if the sellers re-sell the home for less than the amount paid by the buyers, the buyers may be liable for the difference between the first sale price and the second sale price (after deducting a credit for their lost deposit). Finally, the buyers may have to pay the sellers' costs in re-selling the home. This could include the agent's commission, the marketing costs, the legal costs or any other costs the sellers have incurred because of the buyers' default.

Of course, it's generally only heartless sellers who take such draconian action. Fair and compassionate sellers may just re-sell the home — often for the same or a better price.

Be careful, however. If you are the seller and you are kind to the buyers, the agents may not be so kind to you. They will argue that they sold your home twice: once to the first buyers, then again to the second buyers. They may then demand that you, the sellers, pay two commissions.

This risk can be eliminated by deleting the appropriate clauses in the agent's selling agreement (at the time you list your home).

This is another reason why it's essential to get competent and independent legal advice *before* you sign a document. It's also essential that you make time to read every word of any document any agent asks you to sign. Even if they say it's 'standard' and all sellers sign it, not you.

You are a prudent seller. You do not sign anything before you are 100 per cent sure that you are protected.

Safety first is your priority.

# 203 Will my selling agent help me buy another home?

A decent and competent agent will always help sellers buy another home. Often this can save the sellers thousands of dollars. First, from the price of the home and, second, by saving the cost of a buyers' agent.

Buyers' agents are a recent phenomenon in Australia. While many are former sellers' agents, early reports of client satisfaction are more favourable than with most sellers' agents. However, some buyers' agents convince buyers to pay a lot of money that is hard to justify.

> *And here's the rub: If you hire a typical buyers' agent, the more you pay for a home, the more you pay the buyers' agent.*

Imagine hiring a sellers' agent where the lower the price they sold your home for, the higher their commission. It's nonsensical.

Most sellers become buyers. Many have already paid thousands of dollars in needless marketing costs plus a massive commission to their selling agent. And then, when it's time to buy, they waste thousands of dollars more with a buyers' agent.

A good sellers' agent will help sellers buy another house. The agent will give them tips on how to find the right home and will gladly negotiate on their behalf. In most cases, at no charge.

When you are hiring an agent to sell your home, ask them (softly and pleasantly) if they will also help you buy a home. This could save you a lot of money. Particularly if your sellers' agent is a competent negotiator.

And certainly, if a sellers' agent offers help when the sellers become buyers (all at no extra charge), this means that the sellers' agent is likely a good and decent person. Seriously consider hiring such an agent.

# 204 What happens if I can't find a new home before settlement?

If settlement is looming and you haven't found a suitable home to buy (or even somewhere to live), you can politely ask the buyers to give you more time to find a home. Of course, you should offer to pay them a rental amount (a License Fee) if they have settled the purchase. Whether they are borrowing the money to buy your [former] home or they have paid cash, they will incur a cost if you stay in their home. Therefore, at the very least—and in fairness—you should cover the costs of their loan or their amount lost by not earning interest on their capital.

Whether you are selling or buying, it's usually a sensible strategy to meet the other parties. When agents refer to buyers as 'the buyers' or to sellers as 'the vendors' it erases the human element from the transaction. People rarely care about strangers.

Too many agents seem to forget (or never realise) that buying or selling a home is not only a stressful experience, it's highly emotional. Rare are buyers (or sellers) who don't shed tears at some stage. When you empathise with buyers, you create a bond of reciprocity that works in both your favours.

When my wife and I married, she had five words engraved inside our rings. Those words could help bring humanity and consideration into any sale. They are: *Be kind to one another*. Kindness is a gesture that everyone understands.

If the worst happens, you may have to find alternative accommodation. Either a rental property or even a motel. Or couch-surf with family or friends. Increase the love-bond between you.

## Key takeaways from part 11

▶ Once a sale is legally binding, it's rare for anything to go seriously wrong.

▶ Nothing is 100 per cent sure until final settlement has taken place. But only about 1 per cent of home sales encounter a serious delay in the settlement process. And once the cooling-off period expires, fewer than one sale in 2500 ever fall over.

▶ The agents usually get paid their commission once the sale has settled.

▶ As commission is usually taken from sale proceeds, sellers don't feel it as acutely as if they personally paid it. But don't forget that every dollar is still your money at stake.

▶ Delays with settlement are often caused when buyers have trouble arranging their loan.

▶ As a seller, disclose what should be disclosed—ethically as well as legally—and you'll help prevent problems down the line.

▶ Treat buyers honestly and with respect and they'll likely treat you similarly.

▶ If the buyers are delaying settlement, your lawyer may issue a Notice to Complete.

▶ Beware that if a sale falls over, you may still be liable for commission, especially if you, the sellers, change your mind and decide not to sell. And if you do re-sell, the agent might expect *two* commissions. Always check the fine print.

▶ The best sales agents gladly help sellers to buy another home, thereby possibly saving the sellers thousands of dollars in paying a buyers' agent.

*(continued)*

> ▸ If you can't find another home to move into, consider asking the buyers to allow you to stay in your home under a licence agreement for a short time.
>
> ▸ Always try to meet the buyers of your home. And always remember the five words: *Be kind to one another*. Kindness makes for a smooth sale process.

# PART 12

# OTHER QUESTIONS YOU MAY WANT ANSWERED

Having discovered the answers to more than 200 home-selling questions, you now possess more knowledge than most home sellers.

You can now find a skilled and competent agent. You can choose the sales method that gets you the best sale price. You know how to stand firm and reject excessive costs. You know how to let agents take the commercial risks, not pass them on to you. You know the Golden Rule of Selling a Home: *Pay nothing until your home is sold* and you are happy with the result.

In this final part, you'll discover a few more questions that may arise when selling your home.

Please remember, however, that if you think of a question that is not in this book, you are welcome to email support@jenman.com.au. We will always reply as soon as humanly possible. And you will always receive a reply from a genuine human, with genuine intelligence and with plenty of experience at supporting home sellers.

We wish you success with your home-selling journey. We care about your wellbeing, and we are proud to help you get the best result when selling your biggest financial asset: your home.

Thank you sincerely for purchasing this book. We hope it becomes an excellent investment.

## Questions in this part

205. What is the single biggest mistake made by home sellers?
206. What do I say to other agents who call me to say they have a buyer?
207. Do I have to give out keys to my home?
208. What is the best book ever written on real estate?
209. Why should I pay an agent's commission when all they do is put an ad online?
210. How do I sell without an agent?
211. When agents say they support the Jenman principles, how do I know if that's true?
212. What happens if I've got a question that's not in this book?

# 205 What is the single biggest mistake made by home sellers?

The biggest mistake made by most home sellers is *failing to research*.

Consequently, most sellers choose the wrong agent and the wrong selling method. They fail to realise that agents generally work for themselves, not for sellers.

Every hour of research can result in thousands of dollars extra in two ways:

- by saving you thousands of dollars in expenses, and
- by giving you tens — even hundreds — of thousands of extra dollars on the sale price of your home.

# 206 What do I say to other agents who call me to say they have a buyer?

Once you choose an agent to list your home, expect to be contacted by other agents. These stalking-style agents are usually the worst. They are lazy vultures who don't put in the effort (and lack the skill) to win enough of their own listings, so they target other agents' listings.

These agents will undermine your chosen agent. Don't let them sow doubts in your mind. You have chosen your agent. Stick with that agent. Give them a chance to prove themselves.

One ploy that other agents use to undermine listing agents is the 'got a buyer' trick. The sneaky agent will claim they have someone interested in your home, often at (or over) the price you expect. In most cases, such claims are untrue. You should tell agents who pester you (some border on stalking) to contact your agent.

If your listing period is nearing its end and your home hasn't sold, expect to be contacted by even more agents. If your current agent has worked well and you are happy with their efforts, don't change. Most sellers who switch agents get a lower price with the second agent than they could have received with their first agent. Of course, if your listing agent acts unethically or is not treating you well, dismiss them as soon as you can.

# 207 Do I have to give out keys to my home?

Yes. If you trust the agent, give them the keys to your home. You never know when the right buyer might turn up. You don't want to rely on you always being at home. Sure, your best friends probably don't have the keys to your home.

However, if you don't trust the agent, don't give them the keys to your home. Indeed, don't hire an agent you don't trust.

# 208 What is the best book ever written on real estate?

Hopefully, the book you are currently reading.

Since the publication of my first book, *Real Estate Mistakes*, in 2000, I have written several books on how sellers and buyers can do well in real estate.

With more than two million copies published, I suppose the public has a high opinion of my books. However, the fact that so many people are still ripped off in the real estate world often makes me feel like a failure. What am I doing wrong? I have never had a complaint from an honest consumer about my books. The only people who complain are agents, some of whom throw vile abuse. They have never read any of my books.

But one thing I know for sure is this: decent and objective agents who do read my books are supportive. I take great confidence and pride in suggesting these agents to home sellers who ask me for an agent they can trust.

# 209 Why should I pay an agent's commission when all they do is put an ad online?

Thousands of home sellers ask this question. Yet few follow through and find a satisfactory answer.

In many cases, with many agents, sellers would be better off without an agent. Many agents do nothing that sellers could not do for themselves.

In fact, many sellers could do a better job selling their own homes than if they hired a typical real estate agent.

# 210 How do I sell without an agent?

It's the biggest secret in the real estate world. And it can't be repeated often enough. Many agents don't do anything that most sellers couldn't do themselves. Indeed, some sellers could not only sell their home and save the huge costs, they could get a better price than many agents.

Let's be clear: the best way to sell your home is to hire a skilled negotiator. No-one — not even the most confident owner — can get a better price than a skilled negotiator.

If you can't find a skilled and competent agent, you only have two choices: use a typical agent or sell your home without the agent.

Typically, many agents do three things — and that's basically it:

- First, they place an advertisement on the internet. *Most sellers can place an advertisement on the internet.*
- Second, they hold an open house and wait for buyers to turn up. *Most sellers can wait at their home for buyers to turn up.*
- Third, agents wait for a buyer who wants to buy the house. *Most sellers are capable of saying yes to a buyer who wants to buy their home.*

Agents don't *sell* homes; buyers buy homes. And buyers will buy homes whether dealing with an agent or the owner. In many cases buyers prefer dealing with owners.

So, if you can't find a skilled and competent agent, instead of using a typical agent, ask yourself: 'Can I do the three tasks mentioned above?' If so, you don't need a typical agent. Do it yourself.

# 211 When agents say they support the Jenman principles, how do I know if that's true?

One of the most common statements made by agents who want to list your home — especially if you know about my vendor advocacy service, Jenman Support — is, 'Oh yes, we use the Jenman method'. Some claim to be 'approved' by Jenman Support.

Please be careful. Some of the worst agents pretend to support Jenman — or, worse, associate with Jenman Support purely to win business for themselves.

If you have read this book (or any of my books), ask if they've done the same. Ask what parts of the Jenman principles they like. Beware of agents who seem to complicate things or use big words to make themselves look clever. Don't let them be nebulous or platitudinous.

If you are impressed with an agent, *don't sign anything* until you contact Jenman Support and ask for information about the agent. We can make sure the agent follows (at least) the eight protection principles of the Jenman Support system. And it won't cost you a cent. If you would like more information, please email Jenman Support at support@jenman.com.au.

# 212 What happens if I've got a question that's not in this book?

Feel most welcome to contact me at support@jenman.com.au.

Also, I sincerely hope you contact Jenman Support when you need to sell — and before you contact an agent.

Finally, thank you for reading this book. I hope it saves you many thousands of dollars when you sell your home.

### Key takeaways from part 12

▶ The biggest mistake made by home sellers is failing to do basic research. Revisit the questions throughout this book as you work towards hiring the right agent, choosing the right method of sale, paying a fair commission and being treated ethically.

▶ If other agents contact you, refer them to your chosen agent.

*(continued)*

- If you are happy with your chosen agent and the listing time-period is expiring, stick with the same agent. If you are not happy, change agents.
- Be careful switching agents as many sellers get a lower price with a second agent.
- If you trust your agent, give them keys to your home. You never know when the right buyer may want to see your home. (If you don't trust an agent, don't hire that agent!)
- Focus on what's best for you as the home seller, *not* what's best for your agent.
- Typical agents do three things: 1) Place an ad online; 2) Wait at the home for prospects to arrive; 3) When a buyer says they want to buy the home, the agents tell the owners. It's often that simple and basic. You could surely do the same—and save thousands of dollars in commission.
- Make sure your chosen agent can justify their commission. If they can't get a better price than you could get without them, why have them? Do it yourself.
- Agents do not sell homes. Buyers buy homes. Homes sell themselves.

# THIS IS NOT GOODBYE. IT'S 'SEE YOU LATER' — I HOPE

Sometimes, when I reach the end of a book, I feel that I am saying goodbye to a friend: someone who's been on a journey with me for a few hours, weeks or days.

It makes me feel sad.

I don't like saying goodbye. One of my best friends, John Maclean, is a 95-year-old farmer. He never says goodbye. Instead, he says, 'I'll see you later'. And always with a smile that lights up his face.

Having bought my book and having read to the end (I hope), please don't feel that you have to say 'goodbye' to me or my son Alec, who co-authored this book. Alec, in particular, spends most of his waking days helping home sellers. First, to find the right agent and second, to make sure the sellers sell for the right price without needless expenses. You are welcome to contact Alec on support@jenman.com.au if you need any real estate help. Or if you have further questions.

During my lengthy real estate life, I have often received unpleasant comments from real estate agents. Their main gripe is that I am revealing their tricks in my books and articles. In response, I love to quote the writer Anne Lamont: 'If people wanted us to write warmly about them, they should've behaved better'.

Also — as I often tell agents — in my own real estate career, I was never paid commission by real estate agents. It was the owners — the people who trusted me to sell their homes — who paid me. These people were my true bosses. They were then — and they are now — the people to whom I give my complete loyalty.

If there is one common mistake that agents make about me, it's this: they fail to see that my motive for helping home sellers is simply that I want to help home sellers. These people — hopefully you, the reader of this book — are the people to whom I owe almost everything that I have today, at least in financial security.

When I was 17, I left my parents' family cattle station in Central Queensland. I loved that farm, but I wanted to spread my wings — to see the world. My father sold the cattle station after I left. I went to Sydney, got a job in real estate and then later opened my own real estate office. My success led to me teaching agents, specifically, how to sell real estate ethically. No matter how successful I became, however, and no matter how much I earned, I never forgot that, in real estate, every dollar that is earned can be traced back to the home sellers.

These are the people who pay the wages and create the profits — one way or another — of every person who works in the real estate industry. The homeowners are the people who must always matter most.

Exactly 30 years after I left the family farm, I returned to Central Queensland and bought back the farm from the people to whom my father had sold it. I could not have achieved this lifetime goal without the support and trust of Australia's home sellers.

Unfortunately, as I often point out, real estate agents are now the most distrusted group in the business world.

It doesn't have to be this way. You, the homeowners, have the power to change the way agents behave. It's simple. All you have to do is refuse to accept the status quo. No matter how many times an agent tells you 'This is the way it's done' or that something is 'company policy', you need to reply by saying, 'It's not the way I do things'. As for the agents having their so-called 'company policy', you need to have your 'family policy'.

If you tell the agents that you will not accept any terms other than 'payment only upon success' and if you refuse to pay marketing costs (as you should) if your home doesn't sell, then the agent will have no comeback. Stand firm.

Many years ago, my wife found a large wooden sign in one of those knick-knack tourist shops. At the time, our three children were teenagers. My wife fixed this sign to a door in the kitchen.

The sign read as follows: *You have two choices: take it or leave it.*

If you can't find an agent prepared to take your conditions, leave them. Say goodbye.

And then remember the 'See you later' words from my 95-year-old friend.

Contact me or Alec on support@jenman.com.au. We will never shy away from doing what is best for you. Also, we will never charge you any money nor ask you to sign anything.

But there is one thing that we will always do. We will always fight hard to protect your interests.

Thank you for buying and reading this book. I hope we 'see you later'.

And remember, *Don't sign anything!* And … *Don't pay anything!*

Not until you are sure you are safe.

Best wishes to you.

*Neil Jenman and Alec Jenman*

## A story you might enjoy

When sellers ask us to suggest or find a good agent, we always insist that the agent agrees to eight conditions, all of which protect you, the seller. Many times, different agents whinge about one or more of the eight points. Recently we had an agent refuse to agree to point 2 (of the 8 points). Point 2 clearly states *the agent must agree not to use misleading or deceptive conduct.* The agent said to us, 'How can I possibly sell houses if I don't mislead and deceive people?' Oh, this real estate world! Remember, you do not have to accept it. As Nancy Reagan used to say about drugs: 'Just say no!'

# ACKNOWLEDGEMENTS

This is my tenth book. But my first to be published by Wiley. And thanks to the amazing people at Wiley — especially Lucy Raymond, Leigh McLennon, Chris Shorten and Renee Aurish — it might be my best book. The team at Wiley have inspired me like never before. Their advice and suggestions have helped me write a much better book. My only regret is not knowing them 10 books ago.

Ever since I read Jack London's novel *Martin Eden* when I was a young man, I have yearned to be an author. Unlike talking, however, writing does not come easily for me. I have read many books on how to write, including the magnificent *On Writing Well* by William Zinsser. But no-one has helped me — or inspired me — more than the brilliant Sandra Balonyi, the copyeditor of this book. Aside from her talent in making me look a much better writer than I am, it's been her encouragement that has so lifted my spirits. Not only has she spent countless hours editing the manuscript, she has also patiently listened to the many sad real estate stories I have shared with her. Unlike my family and friends, she never told me to 'stop stressing'. I get despondent at times with what happens in the real estate industry. I hate seeing good and trusting people lose their hard-earned money. Thank you for your understanding of my feelings as well as your talent in helping me to convey so much advice and so many warnings to home sellers, dear Sandra. I will be forever indebted to you.

For years, I have been fighting to improve conditions for home sellers. But it was Lucy Raymond who pointed out the obvious to me: there are plenty of books on how to *buy* real estate, but there are almost none on how to *sell* real estate. This book, therefore, is a standout among the legion of real estate books, many of which focus on buying multiple properties so that nouveau-investors can stop work and do nothing for the rest of their lives.

This book is more basic. It's about showing home sellers how to sell their homes for the right price with the least costs and minimal stress.

For more than 30 years, I have fought to improve conditions for real estate consumers. As anyone who speaks out about any industry will know, I have dealt with everything from abuse to threats. Vested interests are omnipresent. Real estate is a multi-trillion-dollar industry where billions of dollars of profit are earned annually — most of it undeserved and at the expense of the community, particularly home sellers, who pay huge commissions and thousands of dollars each for mostly needless expenses. There are 195 countries in the world. I believe that Australia is now the most expensive country in which to sell a home.

What I most appreciate about the people at Wiley is their ethics and integrity. Rather than telling me to 'tone it down' or accusing me of exaggerating the dangers in the real estate world, the people at Wiley have given me enthusiastic support. It is both a pleasure and a thrill to be supported by someone other than real estate consumers. There is a reason why real estate agents are now the least trusted of all professions. And so, again, I thank all the people at Wiley for helping me to help more home sellers.

I need to thank another Wiley author, Adrian Raftery. He introduced me to Wiley. I first met Adrian in the 1980s. He was a 12-year-old boy who walked into my real estate office with his parents, Mick and Mai Raftery. They were 'house-hunting-weary' and, like most home buyers, desperately in need of someone to care about them — as people. Not just another 'commission on legs'. On that day, I made the Raftery family a promise: 'Stay with me and I will find you a home you love'. Several weeks later, I fulfilled that promise. The Raftery family moved into a home they loved.

As a young agent, I learned something about real estate from the Raftery family: there is nothing more important — and no greater honour — than public trust. For the rest of his life, Mick Raftery and his wife Mai sang my praises. Today, their son — that 12-year-old boy who is now in his mid-50s — still asks for my real estate advice. As my wife, Reiden Jenman, tells me, 'Trust is more important than love'.

I have always looked upon real estate as being more about people than properties. So, my sincere thanks to the many sellers and buyers who give me their trust. Helping you to get the best result — whether buying or selling — is what pushes me forward every day. And now, thanks to the amazing people at Wiley, I have the chance to help more home sellers.

Writing can be lonely. To succeed, a writer needs allies. My three best allies with this book have been my noble and decent son, Alec Jenman, my loving and devoted wife, Reiden Jenman, and my dedicated and competent secretary, Debbie Matthews. Without their love, encouragement and support, this book — like most of my books — would be merely a dream.

Most of my learning on how to succeed in business and life has come from my prodigious reading. From literature to history, I learned the true meaning of success from authors such as W Somerset Maugham and Emile Zola — to name (and thank) two of scores of authors and historians who, at the risk of using a cliché, 'showed me the light'.

All my life I have strived to do what's right. I have not always succeeded. But I have always given my best. A phrase by W Somerset Maugham — 'Goodness is the most powerful force in the world' — set the course of my life at the age of 21. My real estate career commitment to work hard and take care (do good) with my clients has never wavered. And now, as a consumer advocate and author, my goal is to work hard and take care of my readers — in this case, home sellers.

But what about the people who take care of me — of which I am fortunate to have plenty — especially as the years go by and new challenges arise. No-one has done more for me than my wife Reiden May Jenman. For more than 30 years, she has taken great care of me. On at least two occasions, she has saved my life.

Since he was a schoolboy, my son Alec William Jenman had one goal: to work with his dad. He has now been doing that for more than seven years. I am proud of him. His real estate knowledge is as good as mine ever was, especially at his age. Thank you, Alec, for your love, your loyalty, your commitment. It's not just me who's counting on you to take over from me; it's those thousands of home sellers who get overcharged and undersold each week. They need you and your eight protection points. I am pleased that more homeowners are now contacting you before they contact agents.

Staying alive is important to achieving goals. And with that in mind, I want to sincerely thank the following people: my dear friend Kesh [Dr Keshminder Singh Brar] from my hometown for your constant care and genuine concern over many years. You're a true hero in our town.

Nurses are people I admire — to the point of loving them. I can see why they rank at the top of the most trusted professions. I have been fortunate to meet many nurses who have left their kindness imprinted in my soul. Especially Beth Kleinschmidt and the loving team at Rocky CCU. I'll keep sending you flowers each week for the rest of my life — which should now be longer thanks to you.

Natasha Berney, you worked all night. Your shift ended at 7 am. You were dog-tired and ready to go home. And then you saw a patient in trouble. For the next hour and a half you stayed and helped that patient, not leaving his side until he was free from pain. And then you went home, asking for nothing. You did what you did for one reason: you are a beautiful human being. I was that patient. Thank you.

Dr Lina Ivert, your vivacious spirit is inspirational. Thank you for never giving up on me. And Merrin Thanopoulos, thank you for coming to my aid with your warm and wonderful care. And few people give care and comfort to the sick more than Pastor Paul O'Keefe. You have my deep admiration.

Dr Sam Sidharta, I have not forgotten your eloquence and kindness. Nor have I forgotten how Professor John Thompson saved me many years ago. I am one of thousands of people who are alive today thanks to the dedication of you and all the dedicated team at the Melanoma Institute.

My three best mates, John Birkett, Michael Kies and Jim Grigoriou, I owe you all so much. Just to think of you lifts my spirits. Thank you for your decades of friendship, love and support.

To the real estate agents who do support me, thank you so much. I am especially grateful to those Jenman Approved agents, most of whom have stuck with me for more than 25 years.

And to all those agents who claim to be honest, I urge you to abandon and then speak out about unethical practices. You can't claim to be honest if you continue to support methods such as VPA and underquoting. To profit from the losses of your clients is never an honest way to do business. To remain silent is often considered worse than committing the wrong you witness. At best, it's collaboration — and cowardly.

To those growing number of agents who are now realising that placing the interests of their clients ahead of their own interests is the fastest and best way to succeed, you have my admiration and support. I will continue to recommend you to sellers who ask for an honest and competent agent.

In Melbourne, I sincerely thank the magnificent Steve Ciric who not only treats me, and my family, so superbly well but also looks after all my friends. You are a treasure, Steve. Thanks to you, our Melbourne home feels like home-sweet-home. And, of course, my dear friend, the aging rock star from Goanna who has kept the joy of his youth, Ian Morrison. You're a 'solid rock' to all who are fortunate enough to know you. Your courage astounds us all. Hang in there, mate, we love you.

Back home on the farm, I thank our wonderful team who proudly wear their 'Alchera' shirts while under the guidance of Freddy Brandt, the best ever addition to the Alchera team. His wife Teena brings joy to her job. So too my youngest son, Harry Alfred Jenman, who loves his life in the bush.

I am grateful that all six of my now adult children spoil me — to varying extents. Thanks, kids. I tell you often how much I love you. My first born, Lloyd Robert Jenman, has faced many challenges in his life. But his character should see him through. I have huge hopes for you, Bobby.

The folk in my hometown in Central Queensland offer me love, laughter and enduring kindness. From my neighbour, Lex Webb, who I've known since the 1960s, to my dear friends such as John Maclean, his daughter Cathy and their wonderful family, thank you all for making me feel truly at home. And, of course, I had no greater friend in my hometown (and in my life) than Auda Maclean, who passed away (aged 93) on 15 September 2025. Helping you to write and publish your autobiography — *One Life is Not Enough* — was one of the highs of my life. Your wisdom will now live on for many generations through your book. I miss you every day in so many ways.

My talented and enigmatic friend Greg ('Scruffy') Fuller built me a gorgeous writing cabin deep in the scrub among gum trees in the Dawson Valley in the land of the Gangulu people. This is where I wrote this book and will hopefully write many more. 'Fuller's Cabin' has become my favourite place — especially when Reiden is with me.

Indeed, wherever I am with Reiden (which is most of the time) is my favourite place. Thank you again, Wifey. As you whisper to me sweetly and often, 'We is happy, isn't we?' Sure, we is.

There is nothing I love more than loving Reiden. Thank you for marrying me. It was the best day of my life.

And thank you Dr Sacha Kepreotis for giving me the second-best day of my life.

I dedicate this book to you.